"I'm so thankful Ramon Presson has written this book. I can only imagine the authentic hope and real help each person will receive through reading it. It's the kind of book we all need to read over and over! What a gift."

Pete Wilson
Author, *Plan B*

"Presson as a pastor/counselor has had a front-row seat to suffering. In his book, he goes to the mat with God over the *Why* questions of life. He cleverly gives the reader a truckload of cynic-resistant nuggets of hope. Presson brilliantly redeems the 'diary of why' written on the fabric of our souls."

Jackie Kendall, Author of best-selling book, *Lady in Waiting*; President, Power to Grow Ministries

"*When Will My Life Not Suck?* is a rare combination of authenticity, wit, and Scripture-based wisdom. Dismissing the flimsy promises of the self-help industry, this book takes seriously the ugly fact that our lives simply don't look in every season like a fairy-tale ending—but that we also don't need to stay forever in a place of disillusionment and discontent. *When Will My Life Not Suck?* manages to be both thoroughly funny and deeply serious—not to mention eminently practical in its step-by-step approach toward a life of meaning and purpose."

Joy Jordan-Lake, Ph.D., Author of five books, including *Why Jesus Makes Me Nervous* and *Blue Hole Back Home*; Adjunct professor, Belmont University

"Let's be honest. We've all asked this question–Ramon Presson just pushes the question out into the open, precisely where it needs to be. If you want to laugh and ponder and move closer toward life, you will find a friend in these pages."

Winn Collier, Author of *Restless Faith* and *Holy Curiosity*, winncollier.com

"*When Will My Life Not Suck?* is, in Ramon's own words, 'an exercise in perspective.' Walking with Paul, he ushers us into the presence of the living God and confronts us with the truth: the birthplace of *Authentic Hope* is pain. Spiritual transformation is discovered in a lifetime of suffering, brokenness, and perseverance. *When Life sucks*…God is at work. Ramon opens the door. I beg you to walk through it with him. Grasp the hand of the Spirit of God. Prepare for a journey of a lifetime."

Dewey Greene, Author of *Painful Gifts*; COO of Polaris Hospital Company

"Ramon speaks truth from a sincere heart that has been there. He understands and knows how to communicate living through it. You will laugh and cry…and you will be better for it. Ramon actually answers the question he asks."

Doug Dees, Pastor; Author of *Resymbol: A Guide to Rethink, Redefine and Release the Church*

When Will My Life Not Suck?

AUTHENTIC HOPE FOR THE DISILLUSIONED

Ramon Presson

New Growth Press

www.newgrowthpress.com

New Growth Press, Greensboro, NC 27404
Copyright © 2011 by Ramon Presson. All rights reserved.
Published 2011 in association with Eames Literary Services, LLC,
Nashville, Tennessee.

Cover Design: Tandem Creative, Tom Temple, tandemcreative.net

Typesetting: Lisa Parnell, Thompson's Station, TN

ISBN-13: 978-1-935273-80-6
ISBN-10: 1-935273-80-9

Library of Congress Cataloging-in-Publication Data

Presson, Ramon.
     When will my life not suck? : authentic hope for the disillusioned / Ramon Louis
     Presson.
        p. cm.
     Includes bibliographical references and index.
     ISBN-13: 978-1-935273-80-6 (alk. paper)
     ISBN-10: 1-935273-80-9 (alk. paper)
   1. Depression, Mental—Religious aspects—Christianity. 2. Depressed persons—
Religious life. 3. Suffering—Religious aspects—Christianity. 4. Expectation (Psychology)—Religious aspects—Christianity. I. Title.
     BV4910.34.P74 2011
     248.8'625—dc22
                                                                            2010017193

Printed in the United States of America

20 19 18 17 16 15 14 13   2 3 4 5 6

CONTENTS

To Maureen DeLyon
who believed a broken young man would heal and grow
and make a difference with his life and his writing.
You were Jesus with skin on.

To my wife, Dorrie,
who has not only supported the development of this book
but the decades-long development of the author in all facets of his life.
You are grace personified.

FOREWORD

When I read the introduction and first chapter of this manuscript, I wrote the author and said, "Send me more." I knew this was a book I wanted to read. My enthusiasm was fully rewarded: I laughed. I cried. I identified. And now I am encouraging you to do the same.

Not everyone has experienced divorce, the death of a child, or a cancer diagnosis, but everyone has experienced pain. Sometimes pain is worn on the face, and sometimes it is buried deep within the soul. It may have occurred yesterday or thirty years ago, but things happen that trouble the human psyche, and the hurt does not quickly evaporate.

If pain is not confronted, it can steal all of life's joy. That is never God's desire. Pain that has been processed yields nourishment for the soul. Most of us need help in how to process the hurt. We get bogged down in the suffering and life becomes unproductive.

Ramon Presson has the unique ability of unveiling the hurt and pointing the way to hope. This book is not designed to be a fast fix. It is rather a book about truth that sheds light on pain. It is a book about encountering God when he seems to be hiding.

The book is written not from an ivory tower, but from the trenches of life. While Ramon is a professional counselor, you will not be given psychological jargon. Rather you will feel the pain of a real person who writes out of life's struggles. My experience has taught me that the people who write best write honestly. Here you will read truth that is couched in reality and expressed in candor. Truth always leads to hope and freedom.

Gary Chapman

ACKNOWLEDGMENTS

I'd like to thank the following people for their contribution to this project: John Eames, my agent, was the first to believe in this project, and he walked with me through the process from proposal to completion. Karen Jacklin Teears and Mark Teears at New Growth Press enthusiastically championed the book's message and embraced the title that others wanted to change. Jonathan Rogers, my editor, kept improving the manuscript with his insights and attention to detail. Barbara Juliani expertly guided the book through the maze and obstacle course of publication, and Nick Darrell did the tedious work of copyediting.

Thanks also to Cheryl White and Tom Temple for believing that while you can't judge a book by its cover, if a book doesn't get your attention its message remains completely hidden.

When writing something that contains so much of my own spiritual journey, I'm moved to thank some of the many strategic people God used to shape that journey: Lea Hadden, Mark Corts, Gary Chapman, Don Mann, and Ken Smith. I'm indebted to authors who mentored me from afar: Calvin Miller, Ken Gire, Philip Yancey, John Fischer, Frederick Buechner, and Brennan Manning. A writer never forgets the ones who affirmed his gifts early and urged him to put his thoughts in print: Maurice Thomas, Calvin Miller, and Bill Keith. That list of early and constant encouragers must also include my parents, Frances Presson and

Richard Presson, who believed a third grader possessed a special gift with words and are convinced the Pulitzers are rigged because I don't have one.

Lastly, I'd like to thank my sons, Trevor and Cameron, for helping me to get a glimpse of what the Father's love for me is like. I secretly love each of you the most.

INTRODUCTION

I remember when my father asked me what the title of my new book was. After I told him, I checked my cell phone to see if I'd lost the signal; there was a prolonged silence on the other end. "Dad, are you there?" Dad finally responded, "Is that really the title?"

The title of this book raised a few eyebrows and even scared off a few publishers who were big fans of the manuscript. Several wanted to tame it to When Will My Life Not Stink? So why didn't I change the title? I certainly don't want to shock or offend anyone, but I just couldn't change it after hearing people's reactions: "When's it coming out? I need that book now!" and "Put me down for two copies." And that was before I even told them what the book was about! The title clearly resonated with the many people who have silently or not so silently uttered this phrase in exasperation.

As you'll see in chapter 1, the title originates from the actual cry of a sophisticated lady in a conservative women's Bible study. Without realizing it, this honest woman expressed the question and sentiment of a multitude. Not only a multitude of women just like her, but people different from her in every way. In contemporary slang, she was declaring the universal and timeless question about the human condition. Will my life ever be better than this? Is this as good as it gets? When will my life not suck?

People who know I like race cars are often surprised to learn that I hate roller coasters and would rather have my teeth pulled without novocaine than ride Space Mountain. I like speed, but I like it in long, looping, flat circles, and I like to be in control. I want to drive. If I had lots of money, corporate sponsorships, good life and health insurance, and lame competition, I'd be a race-car driver.

I wish my life was more like auto racing. I wish yours was more like that too—adventurous but level, consistent, and with lots of control. But life often feels more like a roller-coaster ride—slow climbs, sudden falls, jerky turns, and someone else in control of the whole brain-jarring romp. When my life feels like a roller-coaster ride, I want to get off. I want to know, along with countless others, when is this going to be over? When will my life not suck?

But it is into the very middle of our twisting, turning, roller-coaster lives that God comes. It is into the ecstasies and agonies of our story that the Bible speaks. The apostle Paul said that if we only have hope for this life, with no legitimate hope of heaven, we are to be exceedingly pitied. But I believe that the converse is also true—if the only hope we have is the afterlife, then we get close to Camus's assertion that the only question man must concern himself with is whether or not to commit suicide. If the only meaning and purpose is to be found through the portal of death, then why even bother with life?

Jesus said that he came that we might have "abundant life" (John 10:10). This statement is not speaking of eternal life in heaven, but pledging a quality of life here on earth. But don't confuse this with something like the quality-of-life index that is measured statistically by the nation's Economic Intelligence Unit. Most of Christ's teachings were aimed at transforming the human heart and, subsequently, lives, relationships, families, communities, and generations.

Likewise, the apostle Paul was not only an evangelist and theologian, but a life coach of sorts. And it is Paul's letter to the Philippian church that has most captured my attention and imagination over the years. Paul's attitude and outlook in this letter are all the more remarkable given the conditions he was experiencing and the gloomy prospects he faced. If anyone was living a roller-coaster life, it was Paul. If anyone deserved to ask and get answers to the question, when will my life not suck? it was Paul. Yet Paul had a different perspective. He didn't seek to escape the roller coaster, but instead found meaning, purpose, and even joy in the ride.

Human life can be so hard that the joy-filled life demands an explanation. Perhaps the joyous man has an easy life or the glad-hearted woman is in denial of her reality. If neither one of those explanations fits the case, then we are left to ask how the subject navigates a potentially harsh and demanding terrain with their joy still intact. That is what I hope to do in this book—offer a reasonable explanation of the joy-filled life. One of my therapy clients once called me a hope dispenser. I'm hard-pressed to think of a higher calling for a writer.

--- rLp ---

1

Is This as Good as It Gets?

Is life supposed to suck? If it is supposed to suck, then I want to trade it in for something else. Exchange it for what, I don't know, but something that doesn't suck.

—Angie, a thirty-one-year-old waitress

Who knew the roof was about to blow off? The setting was comfortable. The participants were familiar. Karla was having a Bible study in her living room with a small group of Brentwood women. I should mention that Brentwood is the wealthiest community in Tennessee's wealthiest county—the ninth-wealthiest county in the United States. These were beautifully dressed and coiffed upper-middle-class women. They were mothers to beautiful children and owners of beautiful homes. By all appearances, these women had it all together.

As always, the Bible study was meaningful and pleasant in a Brentwood sort of way. Here in the Bible Belt, knowing how to conduct oneself at a Bible study is a pretty basic social skill. Karla asked the questions in the study guide, and the women offered up their carefully calibrated answers—answers that would demonstrate sensitivity to "things of the Spirit" without revealing too much or making anybody feel uncomfortable. They were talking about the book of Exodus—the Israelites' ragtag escape out of slavery and their faltering steps toward the Promised Land. It was interesting enough but not very Brentwood. After all, weren't these women already living in the Promised Land?

Becky, a mother of teenagers, suddenly interrupted the overly polite back and forth. "Forgive me if I'm out of line. I think this study of Exodus is all very nice, but what I really want to know is this: when will my life not suck?" A collective gasp seemed to vacuum all the oxygen out of the room. Some of the startled women looked to Karla for a group rescue, while others stared with an awkward intensity into the pages of Exodus on their laps. Then Sandy, who had recently divorced a music industry executive, found her own courage in Becky's willingness to speak the truth. "Yeah, me too. That's what I want to know. When will my life not suck?"

> "Forgive me if I'm out of line. I think this study of Exodus is all very nice, but what I really want to know is this: when will my life not suck?"

Karla had the wisdom not to try to reel this in. She just nodded and remained silent, trusting that God was doing something important, something real. The raw outbursts from Becky and Sandy, not to mention Karla's mature acceptance, gave the other women permission to drop their masks and let their humanness show through. One by one the women hesitantly removed their fingers from the holes in their protective dykes. Walls began to fall. Every woman in the room—even Karla—acknowledged that somewhere close to the center of her being was a question that she had been afraid to ask: "When will my life not suck?"

It was way past lunchtime, but the tears kept coming. The chicken salad and the croissants could wait. These women thought they had come to Karla's house to study the book of Exodus. But they really sought an exodus from feeling stuck. It was a prison break from a suburban misery of mediocre marriages, consuming parenthood, stressful jobs, accumulating weight, unmet goals, unfulfilled dreams, and crippling debt.

In case you're wondering, I didn't make this up. Karla told me about this episode, and it struck a nerve in me that resulted in this book. The feeling that life sucks is not confined to upper-middle-class women—not by a long shot. Over the years as a pastor, a therapist, and someone who can't help but overhear conversations in the next booth, I've encountered a lot of people who feel that life sucks:

- Singles in relationships that are going nowhere
- Singles for whom a relationship is nowhere in sight
- Wives who feel sentenced to a bland marriage
- Husbands who feel expendable at work and unappreciated at home
- Blindsided and bludgeoned victims of a ruthless economy
- Adults devastated by divorce, and children who must testify in family court
- Mothers who seemingly have no identity or life of their own
- People battling cancer, a chronic debilitating illness, or chronic pain
- Addicts and the people who love them
- Single fathers who miss their children, and single mothers who are overwhelmed
- People whose Prozac, Wellbutrin, or Lexapro isn't working
- People who feel trapped in sluggish, overweight bodies
- Parents of a prodigal
- Victims of abuse, crime, or just betrayal
- The poor of Calhoun City, Mississippi, and the wealthy of Palm Beach, Florida
- Public school teachers, cubicle jockeys, real estate agents, and auto workers
- The geographically uprooted, relocated, and transplanted
- People with sexual scars, addictions, AIDS, or other STDs
- Graduates who can't get a job after four years of costly training
- Parents who have buried a child, regardless of age

- Minorities who are underprivileged and disrespected
- You, if we had a chance to talk

GOD ALL MUDDY

If you've seen the movie *Bruce Almighty*, you'll remember the scene when everything comes crashing down for Channel 7 Eyewitness News reporter, Bruce Nolan. He's doing a live broadcast from Niagara Falls when he learns that his rival has been given the anchor position that he has been counting on getting himself. After giving full and colorful vent to his feelings on live television, Bruce is fired and literally thrown out into the street, where his car is vandalized, and he is beaten up by a gang.

Bruce's girlfriend tries to put things in perspective. "Thank God you're OK," she says. At the mention of God, Bruce goes off on a tirade. "God is ignoring me completely. God is a mean kid sitting on an anthill with a magnifying glass, and I'm the ant. He could fix my life in five minutes, but he'd rather burn off my feelers and watch me squirm." "I'm just glad you're OK," the girlfriend repeats. Bruce shoots back, "News Flash! I'm not OK. I'm not OK with a mediocre job. I'm not OK with a mediocre apartment. I'm not OK with a mediocre life!" Moments later, after another series of mishaps, Bruce screams at God, "OK, the gloves are off, pal. Let's see a little wrath. C'mon, smite me, O Mighty Smiter. You're the one who ought to be fired. The only one NOT doing his job around here is YOU!"

That's a hard scene to watch. It's painful to see a person step so close to the line of blasphemy (or perhaps step over it). But the truth is that Bruce echoes the sentiment of many of us, even though we might be hesitant to say it aloud: "God, my life sucks. You're not doing your job!" I often wonder what we think God's job is. I've had to confront the fact that I have mentally written a job description for God. I've had expectations of God that had nothing to do with reality, and that create dilemmas for me when I think God is falling down on the job. They create conflict when I think the Christian life is not working for me. In fact, the phrase "working for me" is quite telling. It puts me in the role of boss. It gives me the authority to decide which results are acceptable and which aren't. We all seem to be looking for a Christianity that gets results. That's the good life, isn't it?

Browsing in my local bookstore several years ago I came across a book that was all about getting "the good life" from God. Maybe it was a good book, but I choked on the description on the back: "The Good Life is a life full of confidence, connectivity, and competence. The Good Life is what God designed for you—a life full of love and peace, joy and success. God has made a way for you to meet him and has created a map for you to follow...God has invited you into his presence and given you a road map to becoming a competent Christian."

> The Bible is more than a wordy version of MapQuest.

A road map? Forgive me if I sound cynical, but I think the Bible is more than a wordy version of MapQuest. Sure, there are biblical principles to follow, but I hardly see in Scripture a formula, a recipe, or "a road map to becoming a competent Christian." Is the best I can hope for being a competent Christian? Here's my definition of the word *competence*: the ability to do something without screwing it up. It means you can do the job at least good enough not to get fired. Wow, that gets my juices flowing. That's definitely something lofty to strive for. But hey, sometimes we'd settle for that, wouldn't we? A competent life that is manageable and working. A Christianity that is manageable; a faith that works. It has to be working for us or what's the point?

The pragmatism that pervades Western thinking and American thought in particular is the idea that if it *works* then it is *true*. Thus if it *doesn't work* then it's probably *not true*. So if belief/faith/church attendance/serving/tithing/having a quiet time isn't improving your lot—if life still sucks—then God is like a busted hair dryer to be thrown away. Faith worked for a while, but it's broken now. So just toss it and get something that works. According to Christian psychologist and author Dr. Larry Crabb, "Modern Christianity, in dramatic reversal of its biblical form, promises to relieve the pain of living in a fallen world. The message, whether it's from fundamentalists requiring us to live by a favored set of rules, or from charismatics urging a deeper surrender to the Spirit's power, is too often the same: The promise of bliss is for now! Complete satisfaction can be ours this side of heaven."[1]

RAPID SELF-HELP

The self-help industry knows that you want it now, whatever *it* is. You need your best life now. Thus the subtitle of Mira Kirshenbaum's book, *The Gift of a Year*, offers to tell you *How to Achieve the Most Meaningful, Satisfying, and Pleasurable Year of Your Life*. So what are you supposed to do with yourself after that year is over? Buy another self-help book? But maybe you can't afford to spend an entire year getting what you want out of life. You need something sooner, quicker, easier. Well, look no further because the subtitle of Michele Weiner-Davis' book, *Change Your Life and Everyone In It* (already a scary title), claims it will help you to *Transform Difficult Relationships, Overcome Anxiety & Depression, Break Free from Self-Defeating Ways of Thinking, Feeling, and Acting in One Month or Less*. Parents will be especially glad to know that thanks to author Kevin Leman they can *Have a New Kid by Friday*.

And in case a month is too long for personal transformation, a well-known Christian author reminds us that *Today Matters* and offers *12 Daily Practices to Guarantee Tomorrow's Success*. Note those three final words that were thoughtfully selected—powerful words that have us reaching for our wallet and strolling to the cashier with book in hand. These words capture what we really want:

- Guarantee: a sure thing that can't miss, and there's no doubt about it

- Tomorrow: overnight my happiness so it'll be here by 10:00 a.m. tomorrow
- Success: usually spelled $ucce$$ but includes many other components that make up the American Dream

This isn't that kind of book. Later I'll address some specific questions about suffering and provide strategies for dealing with it. But for now, let's just be honest enough with each other to admit that we bring certain expectations to the table. We've believed the Ten Essential Truths, followed the Seven Steps, implemented the Six Simple Strategies, applied the Five Principles, and adhered to the Four Vital Factors. We've followed the Path to Promise, the Trail to Triumph, and the Map to Victory—and when none of it seems to work we feel like throwing God out like a broken toaster. We've got sermon notes, books, tapes, and CDs, and our life still sucks.

> I would be disappointed if you finished this book without greater hope and trust in the living and loving God and without feeling that your winding, twisting journey has not just a destiny, but a great purpose.

If you've bought this book with the hope of it being the one that fixes what's broken in your life, you're going to be disappointed. I'm shooting at a higher target than helping you get happy. Of course I want to instill in you a greater sense of hope. I want to encourage you, make you think, provoke questions, make you wrestle, nudge you to look deeper, make you smile, and occasionally even stick a finger in your armpit and make you laugh. I don't have all the answers, and I don't have a monthly tape subscription to anyone who does. But I would be disappointed if you finished this book without greater hope and trust in the living and loving God and without feeling that your winding, twisting journey has not just a destiny, but a great purpose.

In the end, I hope I can help you embrace the mystery of the life God has for you. Or if you can't quite embrace it, I hope you can at least give it a little hug. I'm not going to solve your mysteries. Audiences think they like mysteries when in fact they like *solved* mysteries. Writers and producers know that audiences crave resolution and feel-good endings. We all do. But life is messy. And while God promises to one day make everything right, the loose ends won't always get tied up to our great satisfaction. Yet there is genuine joy available in the midst of the most bewildering and painful of circumstances.

I know. I've been there.

2

My Hero Is in the Slammer

What do I know about a life that sucks? I'm well educated. I have no student loan debt. I've had great jobs in big churches. I have a successful counseling practice. I'm a published author. I'm healthy. I have a lovely, devoted wife and two perfectly healthy sons who are good students and excellent athletes. I have a nice house in a lovely part of Tennessee. I've also been hospitalized for depression.

I know what it's like to look at my life, understand that I'm blessed compared to a lot of people, tell myself that I have no real good reasons to be depressed, but suffer crippling depression anyway. My serotonin and dopamine levels aren't always impressed with my self-talk. So I take a prescribed antidepressant medication every morning to calm the chemical pond in my brain.

In 2006 I decided to play amateur psychiatrist/pharmacist and wean myself off an antidepressant. I was feeling great, so I decided to experiment with gradually decreasing the dosage. (I'm not stupid enough to stop cold turkey.) I felt fine. I congratulated myself on my wise approach to the process, which had the added benefits of saving money and greater ease in losing weight. I was feeling so good that I ran a half marathon for the first time.

A week after the marathon, I crashed. The doctors hypothesized that the endorphins from the months of training for the marathon may have temporarily made up for the absence of the medicine. In my post-race exhaustion, the endorphins took a hike, and my depression awoke like an angry bear that did not appreciate being awakened. Here's a bit of free business advice: when you are launching a new business—particularly a counseling private practice—I don't recommend being hospitalized for depression. It's not great for marketing. I've learned my lesson. Now I take a Cymbalta in the morning like it's a Flintstone vitamin, and I get on with my day.

Okay, now you know that the author of the book you're reading is on an antidepressant and once spent some vacation time in a psychiatric hospital. Am I crazy? No. Get the images of *One Flew Over the Cuckoo's Nest* out of your mind. If you spent a week watching me closely, you'd likely never suspect that a fog sometimes rolls in and obscures my harbor. But like a diabetic or someone with high blood pressure, I have a powerful, threatening condition that I must monitor and manage. Sometimes taking a daily capsule feels like some form of codependency and/or a lack of faith or strength, and sometimes that feeling pummels my self-esteem. But I have mostly come to terms with it, and I am grateful (as is my family!) that the medicine exists and is only twenty dollars with my insurance co-payment.

Some people judge me, but most have been very gracious in their understanding. My transparency about my battle seems to have helped many others feel less shame about their struggle with depression or anxiety, which has allowed them to either seek help or feel better about the help they are getting.

So when I write about life sucking, I'm not writing from an ivory tower. I'm not looking down on my readers, shaking my head at their dysfunction because I have it all together. I've actually become very suspicious of people who act as if they have it all together and deny any past or current brokenness. It's hard for me to trust people who insist they have no wounds or scars. Not that I think you need to walk around with your shirt pulled up so everyone can see the nasty gash on your belly. I just think it helps for you to know where I'm coming from.

WHAT DID YOU EXPECT?

There's another reason I've told you about my personal situation. For some reason we're always surprised when the world doesn't give us joy. I'm like those upper-middle-class women I mentioned earlier. I've got all the things that are supposed to make me happy, but still I often feel that my life sucks. Sure, in my case there's the matter of brain chemistry that provides its own set of challenges, but that's not the point. Even if I had perfectly balanced brain chemistry, the world still wouldn't be enough to give me joy.

> How strange is it that when we ask *God* to bless us, what we want is simply more of the best that the *world* can give?

How strange is it that when we ask *God* to bless us, what we want is simply more of the best that the *world* can give? We want God to bless us with more money, fewer difficulties, more success, less conflict, more opportunities, and more influence. Sometimes what we want and expect from God is not very different from what we would want and expect from a really good president or even a benign dictator.

Consider the crowds in Jerusalem that first Palm Sunday, when Jesus rode in on a donkey's colt. They genuinely believed he was the Messiah, and they were right. However, they were just plain wrong about what to expect from him. With all those "hosannas" and "blessed bes" they were offering a trade. In effect, they were saying, "Jesus, we'll believe in you and follow you, and in exchange you'll exercise your divine power and authority to overthrow the oppressive Roman government and free our nation from its control, which ultimately will greatly improve our lives." The problem is that Jesus never offered such an exchange. When the masses realized that Jesus did not intend to fulfill the job description that they had written for the Messiah, they turned on him. Five days later, "hosanna" had turned into "crucify him!"

Surely, even the disciples were disappointed that their fame by affiliation was slipping. You have to wonder if at least a part of Judas's betrayal grew out of resentment when he realized that three years of traveling the countryside with Jesus wasn't going to translate into a top-floor, corner office with a view overlooking Jerusalem. When Judas evaluated the big picture, he concluded, "This sucks!"

I hate to confess how well I understand where Judas was coming from. I wasn't singing praise choruses in the psychiatric hospital. Yes, I know about the disciples singing in jail in the book of Acts. You'll notice my name isn't listed there. While in the hospital I more readily identified with some of the protest psalms of David—verses seldom quoted by worship leaders or printed on the screen while the congregation sings a praise chorus. Passages like Psalm 22:1-2: "God, God...my God! Why did you dump me miles from nowhere? Doubled up with pain, I call to God all the day long. No answer. Nothing. I keep at it all night, tossing and turning" (MSG). As repetitive as was my question, "God, will you not hear me, heal and restore me?" were my questions "God, how did I get here?" and "God, why did you let this happen to me?"

FIELD OF DREAMS GETS PLOWED

But if Judas represents one way to react to the realization that life sucks, the apostle Paul represents another way, a better way. If ever there was a man who had reason to expect a different kind of life from the one he got, surely it was Paul. And yet joy echoes through everything Paul wrote—even the letters he wrote during confinement. Paul of Tarsus had a dream of going to Rome as a preacher. In the year 62 AD, he finally made it to Rome—but not as a preacher. He was a prisoner of the empire. No doubt he had pictured himself in the great city as an open-air evangelist, telling people the good news about God's love for them. Instead he found himself in Roman custody, chained to a rotation of irritated guards.

This wasn't in the script. Where were the rewards for radical obedience to God? Yes, Jesus promised that his followers, especially the obvious ones, would be persecuted. Everywhere Paul went he provoked either revivals or riots. But God could have prevented this if he had wanted to. What good was accomplished by having Paul on the sidelines and not in the game? Can you think of anyone during the first century who was a more blistering testimony for Christ than Paul?

After forty-nine years, I know myself pretty well. I can safely say that if I had been Paul (and it's a good thing for Christendom that I was not), I would have evaluated the gap between my impressive résumé of outstanding Christian service and my current incarcerated reality and concluded, "This sucks!"

PAUL'S SURPRISING HABIT

Paul was in that Roman prison when he wrote the letter that we now call Philippians. It is this ill-placed inmate who exhorts the Philippians to "Rejoice in the Lord. I will say it again: Rejoice!" (Philippians 4:4). The writers of yesteryear didn't use a bolder print, all capital letters, underlining, larger font size, italics, or exclamation points to emphasize a phrase. Instead, they used the literary technique of repetition. For example, "Holy, holy, holy is the Lord Almighty" (Isaiah 6:3) or "Truly, truly, I say to you…" (John 16:20 NASB). Paul is here using that same literary technique of repetition for emphasis. "Rejoice. I will say it again: Rejoice!"

In addition to emphasis, this use of repetition counters the skeptical reaction of his audience to his first exclamation. Facing great difficulty themselves and with their leader in prison, the Philippians would likely greet his joyful advice with disbelief or resistance. The repetition is Paul's way of saying, "Yeah, you heard me right; rejoice, I tell you!" This exhortation to rejoice in the Lord comes from a man for whom suffering is not only a part of his past, but a fixture in his present and a certainty in his future. Incarcerated in Rome, awaiting trial before Caesar, Paul is not able to visit the Philippian church. Instead, he must rely on reports, either from a short list of approved visitors like Epaphroditus and Timothy, or written correspondence from the church. Paul is permitted to write, and he certainly cannot be stopped from praying, but undoubtedly at times he feels his ministry is as confined and limited as he is. Nevertheless, as is evident in this letter to the Philippians, his needle seems rather set in a groove of ironic rejoicing.

How seriously does Paul take this idea of always rejoicing? You'll notice that "Rejoice in the Lord always" is a command; that word *rejoice* is the Greek word *chairo*, and Paul uses it in the present imperative tense—like the old Nike slogan, "Just do it." Paul calls not for a Teflon-coated heart that real and valid pain can't stick to, but for a heart that is anchored in reassuring truths and therefore possesses a joy that holds steady whether circumstances are favorable or adverse. How much joy is oozing out of Paul's letter to the Philippians? In one form or another, he uses the word *rejoice* seven times. He uses the word *joy* six times. In a letter that doesn't even take up five pages in your Bible, that's a lot of joy!

Was Paul just in a really good mood when he wrote this letter? Was he bipolar and writing on a manic day? I'm sure Paul had his bad moments and his better moments, but the authenticity of his positive attitude shines through despite the various contexts and issues of the letter.

CANDID CAMERA

When Paul wrote his letters, he was not trying to meet a publisher's deadline or fulfill the obligations of a book contract. Paul didn't have a literary agent steering him toward more marketable content. No publicist was lining up a book tour, speaking engagements, signings at Barnes and Noble, or interviews on Christian radio and *The 700 Club*. Nobody was telling Paul that if he spun these letters just right he could develop a series of small books that would outsell the *Left Behind* convoy.

No, I'm confident that Paul never imagined that anyone besides the Philippians would read this letter. While Paul chose his words carefully, and while I believe that he was writing under the inspiration of God's Spirit, I don't think Paul ever said to himself, "I've got to be careful here. After all I'm composing Scripture that will one day be translated into hundreds of languages and dialects and offered in the KJV, NKJV, RSV, NRSV, NASB, NIV, TLB, NLT, and BLT." Paul wrote with no audience in mind except the one the mailman was delivering the package to. The fact that the content of his letters is totally relevant and applicable to an ancient tribe in Botswana or to a Gen-X church in Boston is a testimony to the staying power of truth.

As you read the letters of Paul, you are not reading the words of a religious spin doctor or the calculated verbiage of a politician's speechwriter. You are reading the words of a man writing from his heart and his gut. It's like finding a stack of your parents' love letters in the attic several weeks after your mom's funeral. You are eavesdropping on an intimate conversation. You are watching a video clip of a hidden camera in Paul's cell. You are sitting in on the class of a brilliant professor who is not seeking to impress his students with his superior intellect, but nevertheless astounds them with his exceptional understanding and his ability to explain the vital verities of life.

In his book, *You Gotta Keep Dancing*, Tim Hansel included some excerpts from his journal entries. He mentioned that allowing others to read your journal provokes awkwardness akin to having someone look through your underwear drawer. In Paul's letters, especially Philippians, we are tossing about the apostle's laundry, and after reading the entirety of Paul's letters, the poor guy has no secrets left. With every passage from Philippians that we peel off and overlay on our own lives, please keep in mind that this letter is the candid photo of a man engaging God in the crucible of life.

Paul's positive attitude is what makes his prison epistle to the Philippians all the more extraordinary. Much of this book you're reading will draw from the remarkable attitude and teaching found in Paul's short but powerful letter. The book of Philippians contains the most worn, underlined, highlighted, and marked-up pages in my personal Bible. When I need an attitudinal front-end alignment—which is often—I turn to Philippians. When I catch myself drifting toward discouragement, hopelessness, resentment, and self-pity, I swim back to the anchored dock of Paul's short letter. I am not outwardly cynical, but as a subtle whiner and a sneaky complainer I am a repeat offender. I often have to turn myself in to Philippians for rehab.

> There must be a lot of people like me running around out there—people who can't shake the idea that the universe owes them more than they're getting.

PAUL'S STRANGE WISH

There must be a lot of people like me running around out there—people who can't shake the idea that the universe owes them more than they're getting. How else can you explain the runaway success of Rhonda Byrnes's best seller *The Secret*. It may have been the most brilliantly marketed collection of fluff and error I've ever read. The secret of *The Secret*, in a nutshell, is this: just fix your mind, thoughts, and wishes on health and wealth, and the universe will overnight it to you in a gift-wrapped package. Byrnes calls it "the law of attraction," yours for only $24.95.

So, if you're a big magnet, what is it that you hope to attract? I can tell you what Paul wanted to attract. It wasn't wealth, weight loss, a job promotion, or healing from psoriasis. In Paul's words, he wanted "to know Christ and the power of his resurrection and the fellowship of sharing in his sufferings, becoming like him in his death, and so, somehow, to attain to the resurrection from the dead" (Philippians 3:10–11).

I'm totally on board with Paul's first two desires: knowing Christ and experiencing his power—that sounds like great stuff. But what about number three, the fellowship of sharing in his sufferings? Are you kidding me? What kind of present on your Christmas wish list is that? Give me a gift like that, and I'm on my way to God's customer service desk trying to exchange it for a package of Christian blessings. Was Paul a masochist or a glutton for punishment? No, the attraction of the suffering was the fellowship with Christ it produced. Paul wanted the intimacy that comes when two people share a profound experience. Who can connect with a parent who has lost a child quite like another parent acquainted with such grief? For a cancer patient, whose fellowship is more meaningful than a close family member who has survived cancer?

Several years ago I felt terribly misunderstood and unfairly judged by someone in my church. How could my altruistic motives, genuine efforts, and substantial sacrifice of time on behalf of this person be perceived through such a distorted lens? When I didn't meet this person's expectations, I went immediately from hero to villain. I wished I could have just shrugged off the e-mail attack, which was copied to several of my colleagues, but it was hurtful and maddening.

One afternoon, when I was walking to my car still stirring the rancid stew of unfair treatment in my mind, I felt as if Christ sidled up next to me and said, "Ramon, I sort of know what it feels like to be blindsided by unjust condemnation. I've had some experience with being misunderstood and judged. Want to tell me about it?" In the car, I mumbled my version of the story and cycled through my spectrum of feelings.

Then I considered Jerusalem's Jekyll-and-Hyde worship turned rejection of Christ. In that moment I felt a comfort and closeness to Christ that is difficult to describe. It is a powerful human sensation to feel deeply understood by another. I felt understood and drawn into the presence of him who experientially understood me.

Keep in mind that Paul isn't suggesting we seek opportunities to suffer for the sake of closer friendship. I doubt that Paul would have commended the religious eccentrics throughout the ages who ripped their own flesh with whips to punish themselves for sin or to win extra points with the suffering Savior. To those misguided souls who during Passion Week have had their hands actually nailed to a replica cross, I think Paul would have retorted with irritation, "When I said 'I've been crucified with Christ' that is *not* what I meant!" Paul neither delighted in suffering nor went shopping for it.

> Paul's repeated request for relief from pain in no way diminishes his legend in my eyes. On the contrary, Paul's acceptance of his unhealed condition inspires and challenges me.

In 2 Corinthians 12, Paul speaks of a "thorn in the flesh" (v. 7 NASB)—an affliction that has provoked speculation from Bible scholars and preachers for centuries. Was it a chronic physical ailment or an emotional weakness? Regardless of the thorn's true identity and symptoms, Paul reveals that on three separate occasions he fervently prayed for this affliction to be removed. It was not. Paul writes that God answered, "My grace is sufficient for you, for my power is made perfect in weakness" (v. 9).

I know myself. If that was the answer I was given, I would have come back with, "Is there anyone else there I can talk to?" That's one of the problems with God—there's not any authority over him to complain to or appeal a ruling. Paul's repeated request for relief from pain in no way diminishes his legend in my eyes. On the contrary, Paul's acceptance of his unhealed condition inspires and challenges me. It is an afflicted man who urges the Philippians to "Rejoice in the Lord always" (Philippians 4:4). Always. It is easy to rejoice in the Lord when things are going well (though it brings up the question, is one rejoicing in favorable circumstances, or in the Lord?). It is quite another feat to rejoice in the Lord when life sucks. What keeps Paul from being knocked off-center by his crummy conditions? It is his intentional focus upon the glory, the goodness, the grand purposes, and the love of God.[2]

> God's promises are different from the promises of the self-help industry.

In contrast to our pill-popping world that seeks a filled prescription for our ailments, Paul seems determined to respond rightly to his suffering rather than eliminate it. I am unfamiliar with that bent of thinking. I'm not saying I run from my problems; I just want them to flee from me! I'm an escape-hatch seeker and an ejection-button pusher. Any part of my life that I feel is subpar is unacceptable. I want my best life now! But God's promises are different from the promises of the self-help industry.

A CLOSING THOUGHT

I have a quote laminated on a small card and taped to my car's dashboard: "Your attitude is either your best friend or your worst enemy." It's a reminder that I can choose who drives. Too often my attitude is akin to a suicide bomber that blows up my joy. As if it wasn't enough to detonate my own day, the shrapnel too often hits my wife and sons. (I usually shield nonfamily members from the fallout. Have you noticed that most people won't put up with your junk like family does?) I sometimes overreact negatively to the slightest of provocations, or I withdraw so everyone will leave me alone. Then when I come home I wonder why nobody's rushing to the front door squealing with delight, "Daddy's home!"

Throughout this book we will be challenged by a man whose physical condition, environment, and circumstances make many of our complaints seem petty. On the other hand, I realize that many of you have faced or are facing extraordinary stressors, physical afflictions, losses, abuses, or emotional pain on a level with which Paul was not acquainted. But I plead with you not to disqualify Paul from having the right to speak into your story.

In the introduction to his biography, *The Sacred Journey*, Frederick Buechner reveals the main reasons he was sharing his personal epic. "My assumption is that the story of any one of us is in some measure the story of us all."[3] There is both delight and plight common to the human condition, a mixed blessing that we all understand; an in-the-same-boat reality that transcends continents, cultures, centuries, and conditions. Moreover, there is an ancient wisdom that transcends all four, and an imprisoned prophet willing to share it. I hope that you'll grant him an audience.

3

Dancing with the Scars

When life sucks, it helps to have friends. I like to imagine the apostle Paul sitting in Roman confinement, preparing to write a letter to his beloved friends back in Philippi, picturing their faces one by one. Epaphroditus had traveled all the way from Philippi to Rome to visit Paul in jail. Lydia, the seller of purple cloth, was Paul's first convert in Europe. The jailer Paul first met when he spent a night in the Philippi jail was now a brother in Christ. Even Euodia and Syntyche, who couldn't seem to get along with one another, were remembered with great love. Those faces and many others were surely in Paul's mind as he wrote, "I thank my God in all my remembrance of you, always offering prayer with joy in my every prayer for you all" (Philippians 1:3–4 NASB).

Are there people in your life about which you can say, "I thank my God in all my remembrance of you"? Whenever I read that verse, I think of an old friend named Maureen. She came into my life at a time when life really sucked—when, frankly, I wasn't sure life was worth living.

Maureen and I could hardly have been more different, but her friendship pulled me out of a ditch that I was having a hard time climbing out of by myself. My every memory of her is spiced with genuine gratitude.

*   *   *

I'm the one who broke off the engagement with Linda, but I'm also the one who fell apart almost immediately afterward. I panicked. I pleaded for reconciliation. I was turned down. That's when I began skinny-dipping in quicksand.

I should have at least waited until after the holidays to break off the engagement. In my rational moments I knew it was the right and necessary thing to do. My heart, however, was protesting and resisting my head's verdict and plan. I could not foresee the devastating loneliness that would take the place of a conflicted relationship. I spent Christmas day completely alone. Family was out of range. I didn't tell them or my friends about my recent breakup.

In 1982 I certainly did not consider myself dependent on Linda or anyone else. In fact, as an only child I took a certain amount of pride in being relational, social, and friendly, but quite self-sufficient. During our two-year relationship, Linda and I minimized, perhaps even ignored, some key compatibility issues. It seemed a small enough price for the privilege of being in love. We often did not bring out the best in each other, and we did not do conflict very well. Let me own that—*I* did not do conflict very well. I was unaccustomed to feeling anger, and I expressed it like a poorly trained novice. My insecurities reared their ugly heads as distrust, suspicion, and accusation. Looking back, I dispensed grace and forgiveness in mere droplets while wielding the past as a weapon.

It was our last semester at Wake Forest University, and we both needed a physical education credit so we registered for ballroom dancing together. Big mistake. When you're not getting along anyway, the failed attempts to coordinate dance steps give ample opportunity to express frustration. Our inability to keep a rhythm and stay in step was a visible metaphor of our underlying relationship. "I lead with the left, we tap-tap with the right, and turn. Is that so difficult?" We were masters at sarcasm. Plus, dancing can be almost like karate if you do it right: "Don't worry about my toes. I can always get new ones." "Nice move—just trip me next time!" "Stop squeezing my hand so hard!" I think we managed a B for the course, but our relationship was getting a C- on a regular basis.

> My experience and my counseling practice convince me that the rope that pulls you out of the depths of depression is a thick cord woven of many important strands.

When I broke off our engagement and ended our relationship, I did not realize that I had just pulled out the stabilizing block from my emotional Jenga puzzle. While Linda was very hurt and angry, she did not attempt to resist my decision or change my mind. While I expected to feel sad after ending an intense two-year relationship, I also thought I would experience some relief, the kind of relief that weary soldiers might feel when a battle is over.

Relief apparently missed its flight because, best I could tell, it never arrived. I soon discovered the fullness of my dependency. I hadn't realized it, but by pressing Linda to be the focal point of my world, I was walking on a tightrope without a net. When I broke the engagement the line snapped, and I inevitably fell. But as Tim Hansel often remarked about his mountain climbing accident, "Falling is actually not all that painful; it's hitting the bottom that really hurts."[4] Tell me about it.

Isolation fuels loneliness and depression, then depression promotes further isolation. Despite my loneliness I didn't feel like being around other people. I didn't feel like pretending everything was okay. I didn't feel like being the life of the party, telling stories, and making people laugh. When depressed you tell yourself things like, "I sure as heck ain't enjoying my company; I don't know why anyone else would."

I don't believe there is a magic pill or a silver bullet for depression. My experience and my counseling practice convince me that the rope that pulls you out of the depths of depression is a thick cord woven of many important strands. One of those strands is meaningful relationships that are supportive and encouraging. One of depression's wicked tricks is to encourage you to talk yourself out of doing the things that would help you lift the funk. You talk yourself out of even trying to do activities that you previously enjoyed. You convince yourself that if you forced yourself to do them it wouldn't help. You tell yourself that meeting a couple of friends for lunch this week isn't going to cure your depression. And you're right. One sociable lunch gathering isn't going to magically alleviate your depression any more than one gym workout is going to give you flat abs. But when you convince yourself of the "uselessness" of small steps and positive actions, you believe depression's lies and unwittingly strengthen its grip. You don't resist depression's gravity, so it gladly keeps you in bed or on the couch where loneliness, boredom, and lethargy conspire with depression to absolutely immobilize you.

I chose not to resist depression's immobilizing force. In 1983, during the dead of winter, I hibernated, coming out of my cave only to go to work. It's a good thing I had a job. That job was the one thing that made me get out of bed, take showers, get dressed, and leave the house. Some people eat more when they are depressed. Some eat less. I had no appetite. My taste buds craved no food that I would have to eat alone. I certainly didn't have the energy or motivation to cook anything. Small portions of cereal, frozen dinners, and canned spaghetti were my staples, along with occasional fast-food takeout. I always ate in front of the television. Perhaps it was my way of hearing and seeing people without having to actually engage them. I lost about twenty-five pounds on an already slender frame.

Loneliness, fear, and desperation make a man do stupid things. Pride goes right out the window, and there's little concern about making a fool of oneself if there's hope of relief. I wanted Linda to take me back. I wanted her to talk to me. I wanted to hear her voice. I wanted to plead, pledge, grovel, promise, confess, beg, vow, guarantee, or whatever it took to get her back. None of it worked. I was like the rat in the Skinner box hysterically pressing the bar after the food pellets were gone. When calm and rational bar pressing fails to get the desired results, the rat resorts to frantic bar pressing and then tries everything else his little rat brain can come up with. I tapped the bar to get Linda to respond. When that didn't work I tapped more often. I massaged the bar; I sweet-talked the bar; I hit the bar, stomped the bar, and ran around the cage pounding the sides. No food pellets.

How could Linda get over me so fast? If she really loved me, if she ever loved me, she would have been as miserable as I was, right? The fact that Linda was recovering and getting on with her life without me only made me more miserable. There must be another guy. I tormented myself with imagined scenes of Linda with other guys. I feared someone telling me, "Hey, I saw Linda last night with a guy at Tavern on the Green. She looked real happy." I feared running into her somewhere—me alone and looking like crap, she looking more beautiful than ever and holding hands and snuggling her nose into some handsome boy's neck. I reasoned that it would likely be some guy from the psychology department at school, someone she had secretly fantasized about while we were together. He was probably some preppy opportunist just waiting for me to be out of the picture. I could never get Linda's attention to warn her about such vultures, and I couldn't get close enough to re-secure her affections and ward off predators. She wished me well, but she closed the door.

I was resourceful. I went to see a counselor at Linda's church. My goal was to eventually have the counselor coax Linda into a session where our alliance would convince Linda of my sincerity, my unduplicated great qualities, and the wisdom of giving me a second chance. Of course, I didn't tell Maureen that when I went for my first session with her at Saint Leo's. For a trained counselor, Maureen didn't seem to understand that the client is supposed to set the agenda. After talking about me and Linda for thirty minutes without taking a breath, I was ready to talk some more about my great loss and my great need for reconciliation. But while I took a sip of water, Maureen hijacked the agenda and asked me about my relationship with God. I treated her question like a mere speed bump on the fast track of where I was steering the session. However, she forged the inquiry into something like the lever that changes the direction of a set of railroad tracks. Little did I know just before I made the turn that I was at a spiritual crossroads. One option was to go back the way I came and try to recapture the life that I had known before it crashed. Another option was to take a new and unfamiliar route on a journey with an unknown destination and outcome.

I really don't know how Maureen did it. All I remember is her praying over me in a very tender yet firm manner, her matronly Irish accent soothing my anxiety. Even God leaned in to hear her pray. She gave me two books to read before our next session. Neither was about broken engagements or how to retrieve your lover. They were about a relationship with God. I clearly was not succeeding in enlisting a cohort in my fiancée recovery plan. Maybe this was what all protagonists felt like in the final scene of Twilight Zone episodes. As I unlocked my car and sat down, I paused before starting the engine. "What just happened?" I said out loud.

Within weeks the sessions evolved from counseling to spiritual discussions and mentoring, from one-hour sessions at the church to unimpeded fellowship in her home.

Our conversations usually began at the kitchen table with hot tea and Pepperidge Farm Orange Milano cookies. To this day wine and communion bread cannot evoke the same emotion and feeling of closeness to God that I associate with the elements Maureen served. Looking back, I'm convinced that they were indeed the elements of communion that the Lord blessed with his presence.

More than friendship, Maureen had become my spiritual mother. Yet our backgrounds were so very different that no one would have predicted us ever crafting a friendship. I was a twenty-two-year-old kid raised in the South who knew little about Christian expressions outside of my Baptist experience. Maureen was a retired neo-Pentecostal Catholic widow from Ireland. I was learning an early lesson in how a mutual interest in and devotion to God made other "incompatibilities" irrelevant. I was also learning a lesson in the high value of life-giving relationship, emotional support, and spiritual companionship.

After our discussions at the table we'd move to the living room for prayer. Just as a client becomes very still in submitting to a hair stylist or massage therapist, I welcomed the magic of Maureen praying over me. Maureen's prayers were sprinkled with something akin to prophecy, a declaring of what would become true about my heart, my spirit, my life, my calling, and my future. They were expressions of confidence of God's work in my life. This was especially important

> Maureen's prayers were sprinkled with something akin to prophecy, a declaring of what would become true about my heart, my spirit, my life, my calling, and my future.

because I was dwelling in a bleak season of low self-esteem and little confidence. For a while Maureen believed in me enough for both us. Unable to produce much movement on my own, I attached myself like a caboose to a moving train. It was the only way I knew to overcome the inertia of my condition. Over time my heart began to heal, the depression lifted, and my confidence and enthusiasm slowly returned. Like the North Carolina landscape blooming in late March, my future was sprouting buds of a captivating vision.

Though our visits were less frequent in the later months, I continued to visit with Maureen right up until I left for graduate school in the fall. Our close connection was maintained. Five years later when I returned to my hometown and church for my ordination service, Maureen was seated and beaming in the second row. My parents may have been more proud of me, but no one in the building could understand and celebrate with me the full meaning of this moment like Maureen could. Only someone who has been present with you in the journey of your setbacks can fully appreciate the significance of your breakthroughs.

It has been my observation that when we experience the power of God's love, we usually experience it through other people—people like Maureen. Maureen loved God; my own experience of God's love was an outgrowth, a direct result of her passion. When life sucks, you have to have friends. They're one of God's most important tools for reaching us and reminding us what is true and good about our lives and the universe we live in.

> It has been my observation that when we experience the power of God's love, we usually experience it through other people—people like Maureen.

* * *

Just as a parent loves all of his children, Paul loved all of his churches and sacrificed for them. But like children, some churches are easier to love than others. The church of believers in Philippi was an easy church to love. Not a perfect fellowship by any means, but as Paul's letter shows from beginning to end, the Philippians were a source of delight for him. In spite of his undesirable accommodations, in spite of the separation, Paul's spirit is buoyed by mere thoughts of his dear friends in Philippi. He opens his letter to them with a gushing expression of affection. "I thank my God every time I remember you…It is right for me to feel this way about all of you since I have you in my heart; for whether I am in chains or defending and confirming the gospel, all of you share in God's grace with me" (Philippians 1:3, 7). If perspective is everything then note Paul's lead here in act 1, scene 1. The curtain rises on his four-chapter soliloquy with the props of his Roman confinement dominating the set. The prisoner launches his emotional confession not with the words of woe, but of gratitude—gratitude for relationship and thanksgiving to God for human friendship and support.

Paul was devoted to the people in his care, and the devotion traveled both ways. The love, concern, prayers, encouragement, and generosity he received from those same people strengthened Paul. These relationships between Paul and his friends went far below the surface. They were brothers and sisters joined in a common bond of love and united by a single purpose.

That's how it had been for Paul from the very beginning of his ministry. Remember Paul's dramatic conversion? He had made a career of persecuting Christians. He was there holding the coats of the murderers when Stephen, the first Christian martyr, was stoned to death. So when he suddenly declared himself to be a follower of Christ, his fellow Christians were justifiably wary. Perhaps this persecutor was trying to infiltrate the organization. It was then that a gentle Christian leader named Barnabas risked his own reputation, and possibly his safety, by taking Paul under his wing. He believed in Paul and believed God had destined Paul for greatness. Before Paul truly went public with his ministry, he spent years in an informal one-on-one seminary with Barnabas. The very name Barnabas means "son of encouragement." Perhaps it was his experience with Barnabas that compelled Paul to pay it forward years later when he befriended and mentored a new believer and young pastor, Timothy. In his letter to the Corinthians Paul referred to Timothy as "my beloved and faithful child in the Lord" (1 Corinthians 4:17 NASB). Again the encouragement and support became a two-way street; Paul wrote frequently about the source of joy that Timothy was to him.

As stated earlier, while incarcerated in Rome, Paul was allowed to have visitors. Timothy was likely a frequent visitor and undoubtedly a favorite. Because of Timothy's love and concern for the Philippians Paul writes, "I hope in the Lord to send Timothy to you soon, that I may also be cheered when I receive news about you. I have no one else like him, who takes a genuine interest in your welfare" (Philippians 2:19–20). In these two compact verses we see a resource that clearly strengthened Paul's perseverance and his remarkably positive attitude in the face of an undesirable situation and uncertain future: the companionship of Timothy and the family feel of the Philippian congregation.

> I have discovered in my years of counseling that most people can endure almost anything if they are assured of at least one of two things: 1) they are loved *or* 2) the current situation or condition is temporary and will either improve or completely pass.

There are times when a crisis itself is provoked by a feeling of being unloved. That may be why the Bible goes to such great lengths to remind us how much God loves us. In his prayer for the church of Ephesus (Ephesians 3:17–19), Paul says, "I pray that you, being rooted and established in love, may have power, together with all the saints, to grasp how wide and long and high and deep is the love of Christ, and to know this love that surpasses knowledge—that you may be filled to the measure of all the fullness of God." Paul is grasping for metaphors, groping for language, and wanting desperately to say, "I want you to get it! I want you to know how much you are loved by your God!"

Paul later echoes John 3:16 in Romans 8:35–39 where he explains that the incarnation and the crucifixion of Christ are supreme visual aids and constant reminders of God's love. But he goes a step further by informing us that nothing can *ever* separate us from the love of God. As an added blessing God directs us to people with gifts of love, encouragement, and support. The physical presence of their compassion is, to use a familiar phrase, "Jesus with skin on." Timothy and the Philippian church were tangible, flesh and blood expressions of God's love to Paul, just as Maureen was to me.

I have discovered in my years of counseling that most people can endure almost anything if they are assured of at least one of two things: 1) they are loved *or* 2) the current situation or condition is temporary and will either improve or completely pass.

Either assurance has great power and when combined they provide extraordinary strength and endurance.

For Paul, these two ideas are connected. Because he knows and experiences God's love, he is able to view his situation from an eternal perspective. While Paul was in prison he was fully aware that there were at least three possible scenarios that could play out: he could be released, he could be executed, or he could be held prisoner until he died. In that situation a person could easily feel defeated. Of the three possibilities, two are terrible, and even if he is eventually released, he's still imprisoned in the meantime. But Paul doesn't despair. He reframes his situation as a can't-lose dilemma.

> For to me, to live is Christ and to die is gain. If I am to go on living in the body, this will mean fruitful labor for me. Yet what shall I choose? I do not know! I am torn between the two: I desire to depart and be with Christ, which is better by far; but it is more necessary for you that I remain in the body. (Philippians 1:21–24)

For Paul, there's no such thing as an insurmountable and permanent problem. If he lives—fantastic! Christ is with him now, and there's more rewarding work to be done. His perspective comes from his love for God and his love for his friends. Furthermore, as in his later declaration that "I can do everything through him who gives me strength" (Philippians 4:13), Paul is confident that he can, with God's help and because of God's love, handle anything that comes his way. Anything. And if he dies—wonderful! Paul will reside in heaven and see clearly the Christ he loves so much. How in the world do you crush a man with that kind of perspective and attitude?

HOW ABOUT YOU?

In your current situation, isn't there a good possibility that your adversity or affliction is temporary? Unless you're on death row or you have a terminal or chronic illness, you probably have reason to hope that your circumstances will improve. In spite of pessimistic thinking that suggests otherwise, in the midst of difficulties most people are blessed with the possibility that their health will rally, their grief will lessen, their finances improve, or their job picture brighten. During the 1990s I ministered in a federal penitentiary in Florida. I was amazed to discover men serving life sentences with no chance at parole who had reinvented their lives and were managing to find meaning and purpose in a life of uninterrupted confinement. With their sense of identity transformed from despised and jailed criminal to loved and forgiven child of God, they seized opportunities to redeem these lost years by finding ways to help others. And in so doing they were fulfilling Jesus' command to love God and love your neighbor (Matthew 22:37–40), including the neighbor in the next cell.

You may be on the front end of a life crisis. Things may get worse before they get better. Or they may never get better. It is then that the first reassurance that you are loved is so very important. Meaningful, supportive relationships are the life raft after an emotional shipwreck. We must remember that this human love is a tangible reflection of God's original love for us. We should also remember that the love that gives our lives meaning is reciprocal—we receive love and we give love. We can't merely be consumers.

At times simply the yearning to be reconnected with loved ones has enabled political prisoners and prisoners of war to endure years of unthinkable hardship. Trapped miners, sailors lost at sea, and hikers lost in the wilderness have often found the will to survive because of loved ones. It was not the fear of death that kept them hoping and fighting the odds; it was the love of or for another person that made them stubborn in the face of severe pain or sickness, depleted water supply, broiling or frigid temperatures, diminishing air supply, or the urge to give in to sleep. Many people who feel trapped by failure or depression resist suicidal thoughts because they refuse to transfer their anguish to loved ones left behind.

4

Garden Club of Warriors

We don't always have a lot of control over our circumstances. Nobody purposely chooses financial ruin or chronic illness. But we can choose to nurture relationships. We were created for relationship—relationship with God and relationship with one another. Within each of us is the yearning to know and be known. So how do you cultivate the kind of relationships that can get you through when life really sucks?

God neither *expects* you nor has he *equipped* you to make it alone. Relationships are standard equipment, not an optional feature like a sunroof or an extra cup holder. We've been set up. God has hard-wired us to need each other and benefit from one another. Solomon understood this when he wrote,

> God neither *expects* you nor has he *equipped* you to make it alone.

Two are better than one, because they have a good return for their work; If one falls down, his friend can help him up. But pity the man who falls and has no one to help him up! Also, if two lie down together, they will keep warm. But how can one keep warm alone? Though one may be overpowered, two can defend themselves. A cord of three strands is not quickly broken. (Ecclesiastes 4:9–12)

I challenge you to come up with a single movie that does not have the dynamics of at least one important relationship as a central theme. Just try. A movie about animals, you say? The award-winning documentary *March of the Penguins* featured not one human being. And yet the power of the film was in the penguin relationships—relationships with mates, devotion to their eggs, care for their babies, and interaction with other parents.

How about a movie with only one character? Do you remember the movie *Castaway*? Chuck Noland is alone on a desert island. No chance of relationship there. Except that he forges a memorable relationship with a piece of sports equipment. Half-crazed by loneliness, Chuck befriends a smudge-faced volleyball he calls Wilson. Wilson accompanies Chuck everywhere, and he talks to the ball as though it were a living person. In the ocean scene, when Wilson falls off the raft and drifts away from Chuck's reach, I wept in the darkened theater along with the grief-stricken castaway. I told myself, "Get a grip; it's just a volleyball!" It didn't help. Losing the volleyball symbolized a profound loss that we all fear, if we haven't experienced it already.

In his novel *The Old Man and the Sea*, Ernest Hemingway places a fisherman in a small boat all alone in the middle of the ocean. Never an overly optimistic soul, Hemingway created a character, setting, and plot that illustrated man's existential loneliness and futility of purpose. No one can help the old man catch the great fish and once caught there is no one to help him fend off the attacking sharks that reduce his prized catch to a shredded carcass. The brilliant and despairing Hemingway was declaring that life is ultimately lonely and without purpose. It is tragic, though not shocking, that the alcoholic Hemingway took his own life while still in his writing prime.

Dr. Larry Crabb insists that most people who spend lots of money for professional therapy could actually be helped in the context of supportive spiritual community (in spite of the fact that Dr. Crabb is one of the most renowned professional counselors in the world!). In the absence of a supportive network, people turn to "experts." I'm not ready to completely criticize that tendency; after all, I'm a professional counselor myself, and I fully embrace my calling to encourage, support, and give guidance to individuals, couples, and families. Quite honestly, I often cringe when I hear the well-intentioned advice people give their family members or friends. I call it IgI: Ignorance with good Intentions.

Nevertheless, I agree in principle with Dr. Crabb. Supportive relationships are key to personal healing and growth. During the initial session or intake interview with an individual or couple in crisis, one of the things I always ask about is the support system they have in place. Who are they? Are they local? How far away do they live? How often do you see them or talk to them? How much do they know about the situation or your condition? In what ways are they supportive and helpful? What are they doing for you and saying to you?

IN THE GARDEN

One of my heroes, Dave Busby,[5] once asked a gathering I attended, "Is there anyone in your life who would be there within the hour if you called at 3 a.m. and said, 'I really need someone to talk to'?" I realized that I had a short list of guys I would politely call at a more respectful hour and ask if they could meet me for lunch or coffee at a time of their convenience. But 3 a.m.? I was forced to face the reality that I had not cultivated that kind of close relationship. I have several good friends and half a hemisphere of acquaintances. But I was short on what Busby called "garden friends." He was talking about the garden of Gethsemane—the place just outside Jerusalem where Jesus retreated the night before his arrest, trial, and crucifixion.

> Then Jesus went with his disciples to a place called Gethsemane, and he said to them, "Sit here while I go over there and pray." He took Peter, and the two sons of Zebedee [James and John] along with him, and he began to be sorrowful and troubled. Then he said to them, "My soul is overwhelmed with sorrow to the point of death. Stay here and keep watch with me." (Matthew 26:36–38)

If you've ever felt overwhelmed and dreaded the events of the coming day, then you're in good company. Jesus knows what that feels like. But note that Jesus did not retreat to the garden alone. He took his three closest friends with him. After three years of doing life with the disciples, teaching and mentoring them, he felt a special bond with all of them, even Judas. Yet he had an especially close relationship of trust with Peter, James, and John. Only these three men were permitted to ascend with Jesus to the area we have come to refer to as the Mount of Transfiguration.

Among the twelve, Jesus felt that these three most fully understood him. In a moment of personal anguish, he had all the disciples sit nearby (except Judas who had fled to finalize details of his betrayal). Then he motioned for the trio to move in closer. To the eight on the perimeter his instructions were simple: "Wait here while I go over there and pray." He didn't even instruct them to pray but only to sit and wait. To Peter, James, and John Jesus privately discloses at a deeper level than he did with the rest of the group: "My soul is overwhelmed with sorrow to the point of death." Do you have someone you trust enough to lower your guard and be transparent without fearing whether or not you'll be accepted?

Then Jesus said, "Stay here and keep watch with me." Jesus asked for what he needed from them. Can you ask a friend for what you need without profuse apologies? I'm not talking about wearing a friendship thin by constant codependent neediness. I'm asking whether you have the gentle assertiveness to request practical help, support, encouragement, honest feedback, or comfort? I hope you have a friend to whom you can say what a client said to me, "I want to tell you something, and you tell me if I'm losing my mind."

Can you request a time to meet that friend for coffee and a deep talk? Can you ask to do a fun activity together because you need to take your mind off your problem for a while and *not* talk about it?

> Can you ask a friend for what you need without profuse apologies?

As a professional therapist I have studied, trained, and have two decades of experience to draw from. It's a deep well of advice. Yet I find that advice and instruction is not the well my clients drink most deeply from; rather, it is my presence with them and acceptance of them that seems most satisfying. I often feel a misguided pressure to be wise and brilliant for them, to dazzle them with insights and overload them with homework assignments. I realize that often I do this to assuage my own insecurity that clients are getting their money's worth, that they are receiving something from me that no mere amateur or even novice pro could provide. Larry Crabb insists that for most people in need the "center of helping efforts is simple kindness, warm affirmation, and words of encouragement...There is obviously a place for advice, insight, and friendly encouragement—but not at the center. I suggest that the absolute center of all powerful attempts to impact people is connecting."[6]

When two things connect in the physical realm they touch like wires, meet like sections of train tracks, or fit together like puzzle pieces. Objects that connect may intersect like roads or blood veins. This positive connecting does not mean always fluffing up the pillow of comfort. The Bible says, "Wounds from a friend can be trusted" (Proverbs 27:6). While most often the great need is empathy and encouragement, there are times the most helpful connecting experience is to be challenged, confronted, or held accountable. "Shannon, I love you and I know you're hurting deeply because of Mike's actions, but that doesn't mean retaliation is okay."

Here's the bottom line. The great dissatisfaction of your life—the reason you feel that life sucks—may be related to a person or a relationship. Someone has wounded, abused, neglected, ignored, slandered, deceived, manipulated, cheated, betrayed, ridiculed, taken advantage, or taken you for granted. (In case I missed your verb, insert it here: _____.) Consequently, you've become jaded about men, women, friends, co-workers, managers, leaders, pastors, landlords, builders and contractors, salesmen, and attorneys. (In case I missed your noun, insert it here: _____.) You may overreact and say, "I just can't trust people. The only person I can rely on is me." Take that approach, and you will be a bitter person whose life will indeed suck almost daily. Meaningful relationships are one core ingredient in the recipe of a satisfying life.

Harvard professor Dr. Tal Ben-Shahar believes that Hollywood's romanticism places the emphasis almost solely upon *finding* the right person. "Many movies are about the search for love, the trials and tribulations that two people go through until they find each other. Toward the end of the movie, the lovers get together, kiss passionately, and then live happily ever after—or so we assume. The problem is that movies end where love begins. It's the living happily ever after that poses the greatest challenge..."[7] As I'm stressing the critical inclusion of meaningful relationships into our lives, I'm not thinking mainly about potential spouses and soul mates, but about friendships. Nevertheless, I believe that Ben-Shahar's call to cultivate meaningful relationships, rather than the more passive approach of waiting to find them, applies across the board to all friendships. So what are you doing to develop new friendships within the social network you already have? In what ways are you intentional about deepening the friendships you already have?

In his book, *The Friendless American Male*, David Smith points out that women are much more likely to have meaningful, intimate relationships. Men, on the other hand, have work-related relationships or recreational friendships, which only allow casual encounters that seldom go beyond the surface. Smith suggests that men have "buddies" but not deep friends. Our playful sparring with one another over the outcome of a football game, or complaining over lunch about the economy, our company, workload, bosses, and coworkers is hardly the stuff of deep friendships. We're not close friends; we're characters in a *Dilbert* cartoon.

In 2004, haunted by the suicide of a young man he didn't even know, Blake Thompson decided he should let his friends know how much he appreciated them. He invited ten unsuspecting guests to dinner...for an awards show in their honor. Thompson publicly affirmed each friend as having a special quality that he admired and presented them with a plaque bearing the title of their Quality Award.[8] I was so captivated by Thompson's example that with the help of my local newspaper I publicly honored two friends, my boss, my counselor, and my wife with the following awards: Garden of Gethsemane Award, Horizons Award, Great Boss Award, Wisdom of Solomon Award, and There's an Angel in My House Award.

Think of the people in your life who have made a difference in the past, and the people who are making a difference now. What awards would you give them? List five people below and create an award for each of them.

1. _____

_____

2. _____

_____

3. _____

_____

4. _____

_____

5. _____

_____

6. Now, how would you like to surprise and honor those five outstanding people with news of their award? You don't have to do an elaborate awards dinner or get the newspaper to publish an announcement. A card or letter will do just fine. Not only will these people be blessed by your thoughtfulness and affirmation, but your own mood will get a boost as you focus on what is right and good in your life instead of what is wrong or bad in your world.

5

Can Anything Good Come Out of This?

For years I've wanted a compost bin to put in my backyard under the deck. We don't have a garden. Our plant beds are small. We don't grow tomato plants in outdoor containers. To tell you the truth, we don't have a great need for compost, and a compost bin is not the most decorative addition to landscaping. But I'm intrigued by the process of composting. Instead of throwing away coffee grounds or grinding vegetable scraps in the disposal, I like the idea of adding it all to the dirt and grass clippings, mixing it into a raunchy dark stew. I'm fascinated by the thought of recycling garbage into nutrient-rich, life-giving soil.

Compost is death in a container. But compost death is alive, breeding, simmering, cooking up an overly ripe soup that is absolute dessert for plants and shrubs. It is that capacity for death and decay to enrich life that arouses my lust for a compost bin. Perhaps the compost bin illustrates what I've intended to do with the garbage in my own life—recycle it. I would love to take my undesirable, painful, embarrassing, and disappointing experiences, and instead of trying to disassociate myself from them, heat and churn them into some new and useful material. It reminds of a Japanese proverb that says, "Do not waste your pain. Burn it as fuel for your journey."

> Think about what your painful experience cost you (peace, trust, self-confidence, time, money, health, a relationship, a dream). To merely bury it or move beyond it is to some degree wasteful.

When a commodity is very costly, you don't waste it. Think about what your painful experience cost you (peace, trust, self-confidence, time, money, health, a relationship, a dream). To merely bury it or move beyond it is to some degree wasteful. There is much to be learned for your own edification, but you also become an invaluable and credible resource to others.

Composting is an exercise in perspective. Consider Paul confined to his corner of prison. In essence, he was in a compost bin of his own unplanned and undesirable circumstances. But he churned the material and identified something good and eternally rich in the mixture. Paul's perspective was not grounded in merely his immediate conditions, nor was it limited by a focus on his own personal welfare. Because of that, Paul may have been confined to jail, but he was not confined by a my-life-sucks attitude.

If we always see our present circumstances as our definitive frame of reference, we're in trouble. Our daily bread will be disappointment, frustration, and resentment. Our contentment and joy will be completely dependent upon our own comfort and ease. I don't mean to suggest that self or circumstances don't matter. But when we don't set our sights above and beyond our own personal and present concerns, we live like a cyclops with one eye in the middle of our forehead—no peripheral vision.

Every other Saturday I take our paper, glass jars, plastic bottles, aluminum cans, and cardboard pizza boxes to my local recycling center.

I dispose of the two heavy bins of newspapers and magazines first, and then the container of miscellaneous plastics and aluminum cans. I save the glass jars for last. I don't dump them in like I do the other items. The glass jars are the reward for this whole inconvenient trip. I select a midsize applesauce jar and slam dunk it into the pit of broken glass. That feels good! The smaller salsa jar hits the inside wall like a fastball and shatters. Stomping on bubble wrap just can't compete with the satisfaction of breaking some glass...and not having to run and hide.

Speaking of broken glass, that's what a mosaic is—shards of glass collected and artfully arranged. It is this imagery that inspired pastor Erwin McManus to name his church *Mosaic*. It is one of the nation's most innovative churches based in Los Angeles, and the following tells why they chose this name: "The name of our community comes from the diversity of our members and from the symbolism of a broken and fragmented humanity, which can become a work of beauty under the artful hands of God."[9] This doesn't apply just to congregations. Every individual is a mosaic of colorful and diverse experiences and influences that God can arrange into something beautiful. Paul writes to the Ephesians, "For you are God's workmanship" (Ephesians 2:10). You may think "construction project" when you hear that word *workmanship*. But the Greek meaning is something closer to *craftsmanship* or *artwork*. The Greek word that Paul used was *poiema*, from which we derive the word *poem*. God views you—just the way you are—as his poem, his artwork. Does that change the way you view yourself?

Psychologists often speak of *reframing*—the ability to look at an issue or a problem from another perspective, especially a perspective that is more accurate, more complete, or more positive. If perspective is indeed crucial to our emotional, spiritual, and relational health, then reframing is a vital tool. An imprisoned Paul displays a remarkable capacity for reframing his situation, and just as importantly, the will to do so.

Now I want you to know, brothers, that what has happened to me has actually served to advance the gospel. As a result [of the incarceration], it has become clear throughout the whole palace guard and to everyone else that I am in chains for Christ. (Philippians 1:12–13)

Paul is able to see beyond his own undesirable situation, and with his gaze fixed beyond his own chains, he is able to extract something of value from the experience. This is much more than just turning lemons into lemonade. This is a choice to focus on what else is true besides the obvious. I mentioned in chapter 2 that Paul had come to Rome with the intent of preaching about Christ in public forums throughout the city. That noble plan was dashed to bits as it became clear that his house arrest wouldn't be a quick visit to the Roman judicial center. Paul's plan dashed to bits—sort of like that glass in the recycling bin. His shattered plan became the raw material for a beautiful mosaic.

> Paul is able to see beyond his own undesirable situation, and with his gaze fixed beyond his own chains, he is able to extract something of value from the experience.

At first Paul must have assumed that his confinement meant the confinement of the gospel. But in the rotation of guards assigned to keep an eye on him, Paul saw an opportunity. He was supposed to be the captive, but they turned out to be Paul's captive audience. When they were in Paul's company it must have been like having a television that only gets one station: WPGN—Paul's Gospel Network. The guards had hours and hours to ponder Paul's description of his own astonishing conversion experience and the miracles he had witnessed. They were intrigued by his teaching and the stark contrast of his behavior compared to most prisoners. These men were likely going home and relaying impressions and stories to their families and neighbors. "Hey, aren't you guarding that troublemaker Paul? What's he like?" And bear in mind, these weren't low-level rent-a-cops who were guarding Paul. They were the praetorian guard—elite, influential members of Roman society. Paul explains that this meant "the greater progress of the gospel, so that my imprisonment in the cause of Christ has become well known throughout the whole praetorian guard and to everyone else" (Philippians 1:12–13 NASB). Extended face time with these guards was a good way to impact everybody else in Rome. The disappointment of Paul's plight is trumped by his delight in discovering that not even the Roman Empire could dam up the gospel. The dam had sprung a leak, and the gospel was seeping quietly into the culture.

Paul then recognizes another benefit of his unplanned sabbatical: "Because of my chains, most of the brothers in the Lord have been encouraged to speak the word of God more courageously and fearlessly" (Philippians 1:14). Because of Paul's courageous example, a lot of Christians have gotten fired up! Benjamin Franklin said, "The best sermon is a good example." Again, a perceived positive outcome of his plight weighs more on Paul's set of scales than his own discomfort. Once again, Paul is encouraged that Rome has not succeeded in drowning out the voice of the gospel simply by closing his lips. Instead, other Christ followers are inspired to be bold.

PAUL'S DETERMINATION TO EXTRACT POSITIVES FROM A NEGATIVE REPORT

It is true that some preach Christ out of envy and rivalry, but others out of goodwill. The latter do so in love, knowing that I am put here for the defense of the gospel. The former preach Christ out of selfish ambition, not sincerely, supposing that they can stir up trouble for me while I am in chains. But what does it matter? The important thing is that in every way, whether from false motives or true, Christ is preached. And because of this I rejoice. (Philippians 1:15–18)

Do you notice what's going on in this passage? Paul acknowledges the presence of troublemakers along with their activities and motives. Yet in the same breath he says "and because of this I rejoice." You might wonder if Paul is in touch with reality. He almost seems like a guy getting a root canal while on nitrous oxide. He knows it hurts, but he's too happy to care.

Paul's witness to the praetorian guard, the renewed boldness of the Christians who *aren't* imprisoned, and the preaching of Christ even by people whose motives aren't pure all have something in common. In each case Paul is focused on a horizon of meaning and purpose far beyond getting relief for his cramping legs and sour stomach. Paul's passion is explaining and spreading the good news about Jesus. It's certainly not happening the way Paul had envisioned, but it is happening, and consequently, Paul is at peace.

> You might wonder if Paul is in touch with reality. He almost seems like a guy getting a root canal while on nitrous oxide. He knows it hurts, but he's too happy to care.

Rick Warren did us all a service in *The Purpose Driven Life* by reminding us that this life is not all about us. It's not about making sure we get a comfy window seat on the bus to the American dream. I imagine that Paul would be amazed by the West's penchant for navel-gazing. Paul's focus is not on himself but on the higher purpose that his life serves. Paul recognizes that his life is but one cutout—albeit an important one—in a cosmic jigsaw puzzle of a gazillion pieces being assembled expertly by a master designer. He submits to the process and trusts the outcome.

People who have persevered despite overwhelming odds inspire me. I don't mean beating the odds of success in your chosen field, but rather taking the poor hand of poker cards that life dealt you and inventing a new game to play with them. When I was recovering from depression, I latched onto the example of Lance Armstrong. While I'm not a fan of the way he has conducted much of his personal life, I was inspired by his relentless insistence that cancer not have the last word. I had never given a rip about the Tour de France, but during the last two years that Lance was racing, I was right there in the peloton with him, speeding through the French countryside and climbing the Pyrenees. Winning a single stage of the Tour de France is an accomplishment. Leaving Paris not once, but seven times with the yellow jersey and trophy is truly one of the most astonishing feats in sports history. That he claimed several of his titles after recovering from cancer only adds to the legend.

I don't wear caps. But there is one that I wear on occasion, and that is the 10//2 cap Nike produced for their Livestrong apparel line. 10//2 refers to October 2, 1996, which is the day that Armstrong was diagnosed with cancer. Instead of framing that date as the beginning of his death, he reframed and responded to 10//2 as a challenge, as though it were a warrior that had struck the first blow. Armstrong was determined that cancer would not be afforded the final and lethal blow. As he sipped champagne on the Champs-Elysées during his victory march into Paris in his first race following treatment, Armstrong drove a stake into the heart of 10//2 and cancer. And in the 1999 Tour de France, while he was officially racing for the U.S. Postal Service, Armstrong declared that he was jamming the pedals for cancer survivors, cancer patients, and their families the world over. Though uttering few words about the disease throughout the race, he became their spokesman. Yellow Livestrong bracelets were everywhere, and all the proceeds were given to cancer research.

As is the case with any sports feat, ultimately a cycling accomplishment has a short shelf life in terms of its actual impact on others' lives. Armstrong's accomplishment was something much more than a mere sports feat. His determination to extract something of value from the horrors of cancer and the early prognosis of doom dropped a boulder into the pond, producing ripples that touched several shores, inspiring like-minded determination in cancer patients, and producing donations of millions of dollars for cancer research and treatment. It is impossible to adequately qualify or quantify the outcomes of Lance Armstrong's personal response to his own disease.

Paul demonstrated a similar defiance toward the forces that would conspire to discourage him, discredit him, or silence him. Paul had critics even within his churches. The church in Corinth questioned his qualifications as an apostle and gave him low marks as an orator. Lastly, Paul faced constant opposition from the Jerusalem establishment and the Roman authorities. Vincent Van Gogh wrote, "The fishermen know that the sea is dangerous and the storm terrible, but they have never found these dangers sufficient reason for remaining ashore." For Paul neither the obstacles he faced nor the resistance he regularly encountered were sufficient to silence or slow him.

How do you defeat a person who continues to reframe his or her own suffering? The short answer: you can't. As Paul wrote to the Christians at Rome, "We rejoice in the hope of the glory of God. Not only so, but we also rejoice in our sufferings, because we know that suffering produces perseverance; perseverance, character; and character, hope" (Romans 5:2-4). Paul and the early Christians were not as spiritually immobilized by troubles as we often are. Their steadfastness in the face of affliction and their joy in spite of hardships can largely be attributed to their perspective and their ability to reframe suffering. Someone has wisely said, "Suffering is difficult; suffering without meaning is intolerable." Paul's view of life invited God to rip the prison door off meaningless suffering. Though they never put it in these specific terms, the early Christians' actions and reactions indicate that they fully understood and truly believed that God is good, life is not fair, and that God and life are not the same things.

One of the most honest self-help books ever written is Dr. Scott Peck's *The Road Less Traveled*. It begins with one of the shortest and most understated pronouncements in all of non-fiction: "Life is difficult."[10] Upon establishing this simple and unglamorous truth, the remaining pages press the reader, with Dr. Peck's guidance, to answer the question: "So, now what?" It is a given that life will often be difficult, unfair, painful, and illogical. Peck suggests that you can accept that reality and proceed accordingly toward meaning and mental health, *or* you can rail and rage against it, either in toxic anger and bitterness, bottomless grief, or immobilizing self-pity.

It is quite liberating to be able to see beyond the glare of negative circumstances and catch a glimpse of something redemptive while in the midst of a crisis. But the reframe and the ability to extract something of value from the crisis often come later with some distance and perspective. There are numerous things in my life that made absolutely no sense while I looked at them as current events through my front windshield. They only made sense when I later peered at them in my rearview mirror.

As a freshman I had a successful year on the Wingate College tennis team, winning over 80 percent of my matches. Naturally I was looking forward to my sophomore season with another year of experience, maturity, and improved skills to bring to the court. Five days before spring practice began, I broke my right hand playing intramural basketball. If I had to break a hand, why couldn't it have been my left hand? At least I could throw and serve the tennis ball with a cast on my left hand. Why did it have to be my racket hand? I'd played years of full contact sports and never missed a single game because of an injury. Now a broken hand would cause me to miss the entire season.

I was devastated not just because of my lost sophomore season, but because it was going to be my final season. I had long since planned to transfer to Wake Forest for my junior and senior years, and I knew that I did not have the tennis game to compete on the Division One level and in the ACC. When the emergency room physician showed me the x-ray of my fracture, I knew that competitive tennis was over for me. Suddenly a sport that had consumed me since ninth grade was over. Something that I did almost daily for the past six years was now irrelevant. I don't mean to be overly dramatic; it's not like I was an Olympic skier breaking a leg five days before the opening ceremonies. As collegiate sports go, I was small time. The dream to go undefeated in my swan song season belonged to a minor leaguer in Division Two tennis, but it was *my* dream. That dream turned out to be as fragile as the metacarpal bones in my hand.

Maybe I was still in a state of disbelief when I returned to my dorm room after midnight. But I was awakened by reality early the next morning, when in my sleepy stupor I raised my forearm to lay it across my forehead and clonked my head with my cast-heavy hand. Instead of waking up from a nightmare, I felt like I woke up to one. News travels fast on a small campus, and the tennis coach already was fuming over the news when I found him. "What were you doing playing intramural basketball?" It was a rebuke, not a question. He would have to get in line behind me. I had been berating myself well before he showed up.

My English professor, Maurice Thomas, led the creative writing workshop I was taking as an elective. I had enjoyed creative writing since the third grade when I was given some little award for a poem I had written. Dr. Thomas was also the founder and editor of *CounterPoint*, the student literary journal that was published each April. I had landed a few poems in the publication my freshman year and was planning to do so again that year. Knowing my tennis season was over before it had begun, one afternoon Dr. Thomas asked to see me after class. He invited me to serve with him as the student editor for the upcoming issue of *CounterPoint*. I enthusiastically accepted. I could not have known it at the time, but a profound shift had just occurred. From that moment on, writing became increasingly prominent in my life, and tennis faded into an occasional hobby.

During that final semester, my tennis racket angrily thrown into the back of my closet, I held a pencil awkwardly between my thumb and last two fingers and wrote…and wrote…and wrote. The student editor position provided me the opportunity to meet several times a week with Dr. Thomas, reading, critiquing, discussing, and selecting poetry. Often the review and feedback was focused on my own poetry. I soaked up the attention and affirmation, and I welcomed the mentoring to improve my writing. Two years later, as a Wake Forest senior, my collection of poetry won a first-place award from the Academy of American Poets. I was never a realistic candidate as a walk-on member of the Wake Forest tennis team. But as it turns out, I had a gift for writing that found its way to the front once tennis moved aside. Dr. Thomas was one of the first people I contacted with the news.

Twenty-eight years after he changed my life in one semester, Dr. Thomas and I still stay in touch. I send him copies of almost everything I publish with a note reminding him that these are his literary grandchildren. And every April he still sends me a copy of the new issue of *CounterPoint*. When I pull the journal out of its large mailing envelope I hold it like a holy relic because of what it symbolizes for me. I secretly call it *TurningPoint*.

> If you insist that your life just plain sucks, you need to ask yourself what you are overlooking or wasting. Can you see anything redemptive or useful from your past or in your current circumstances?

Hardly a day goes by that I do not write. It's been like that for as long as I can remember now. What I can't remember is the last time I pulled the cover off my tennis racket to smack some top-spin forehands with a perfectly healed right hand. When I tell this story, I am sometimes asked if I think God caused me to break my hand in order to make me a writer. No! I don't think God caused me to fall while I was running backwards on defense. To tell the truth, I'm not especially interested in placing blame. The point of the story is that God was at work in a hard situation to redeem it. God brought beauty out of ashes. He graciously enabled me to redeem the broken season, recycling a semester of what I initially thought was only garbage. The scraps of a tennis dream became the compost where the seeds of a writer were planted.

If you insist that your life just plain sucks, you need to ask yourself what you are overlooking or wasting. Can you see anything redemptive or useful from your past or in your current circumstances? Will you insist upon only viewing your life as you do now, staring it down through the lens of your habitual negativity and refusing to see it differently until something or someone touches it with a magic wand and turns the piles of gunk into gold? If that's what you're holding out for, you're going to get really tired of the magazines in the waiting room.

6

Whenever Whatever Happens

I n a classic *Calvin and Hobbes* cartoon, Calvin regretfully informs his dad that, according to Calvin's poll research, his dad's approval ratings have been dropping as of late. Luckily Calvin has a short list of suggestions for his dad to raise his slumping approval. I've noticed that God welcomes and even craves our prayers but continues to decline to put a suggestion box outside his office. I've known many people whose response to crisis or prolonged dissatisfaction has been to place God on probation or to exile him. When life sucks they write God off. They subtly declare, "When God starts performing better and my life improves, then I'll let him back into my life."

A popular movement in the corporate world is something called "360 feedback." This system involves everyone, including employees, supervisors, upper management, and even the CEO, offering and receiving feedback. The secure and humble company president invites his subordinates to tell him what they really think of him. My sources tell me that 360 feedback is much more popular in business books than it is in actual business offices. God is no dictator, but he's not running a democratic form of government, and he's not the president of a board of directors. No one voted him in; no one is voting him out. He's not asking for 360 feedback and evaluations from his creation. He is asking for faith and trust—faith that he is good and trust that he knows what the heck he's doing.

*   *   *

So you have questions about God's leadership style. You need reassurance that God knows what he's doing. Does that make you a faithless heretic? Not necessarily. Actually, it puts you in the same boat with John the Baptist.

Picture it: John the wild-man prophet is in prison after making unflattering remarks about Herod's second marriage. This is the same John the Baptist who boldly declared of Jesus, "Look, the Lamb of God, who takes away the sin of the world!" (John 1:29). Before anyone else seemed to really understand that Jesus was the Messiah, the Son of God, John was adamantly vocal about the true identity of Christ. If John the Baptist had known Superman he would have blown his cover. "Hey, everybody, Clark Kent is really Superman. Don't let the glasses fool you; he can see through walls!" This same John the Baptist is now in the prison of a madman, and if he fears for his life, you can understand why (Herod eventually had John's head cut off).

If you put yourself in John's place, you can perhaps understand his jailhouse confusion. You are Jesus' cousin as well as one of his closest friends. You've repeatedly witnessed Jesus' miracles and his convincing testimonies of his divine authority and power. Is Jesus just going to let you rot in this dungeon? With all that power and authority why doesn't he bust you out? If you're going to decay in prison or die for your convictions, you may want some reassurance that the cause or the person you're prepared to die for is...well...you might want to be sure that you're sacrificing yourself on the altar of something that is *true*, not something that is just worthwhile. So John sent his own disciples to Jesus to ask a question: "Are you really the Messiah, or should we keep looking?"

Jesus rarely answered questions with a direct yes or no. He didn't this time either. "Go back and report to John what you have seen and heard: The blind receive sight, the lame walk, those who have leprosy are cured, the deaf hear, the dead are raised, and the good news is preached to the poor" (Luke 7:22). Jesus was citing prophetic passages from the Old Testament book of Isaiah. It was a powerful way of saying, "I'm doing exactly what I'm supposed to be doing, what I was brought here to do." Then Jesus added an intriguing statement: "Blessed is the man who does not fall away on account of me" (Luke 7:23). Allow me to paraphrase: "Fortunate is the guy who doesn't freak out over the way I do things."

Not freaking out is really hard to do sometimes. I've wanted desperately to believe what one of my former pastors often said: "God never mismanages anything." But I admit being baffled by God's management strategies. Paul's exhortation to the Philippians offers insight into my confusion. "Whatever happens, conduct yourselves in a manner worthy of the gospel of Christ" (Philippians 1:27). In its context Paul is actually saying, "Whatever happens to me, you conduct *yourselves* in a manner worthy of the gospel of Christ." Paul exhorted the Philippians to hold his current situation and future outcomes in a proper perspective as it related to them. Paul was telling them that even if he was executed, they were still responsible for their own actions, reactions, and attitudes. Even if his life were cut short, their lives were to continue to be extraordinary. Essentially Paul was saying to them, "Don't even think about using my imprisonment or death as an excuse to give up and go AWOL."

> I've wanted desperately to believe what one of my former pastors often said: "God never mismanages anything." But I admit being baffled by God's management strategies.

I want to believe that God never mismanages anything, but I have trouble sometimes reconciling this concept with global disasters and next-door tragedies. Sometimes it's hard not to view miscarriages, foreclosures, layoffs, traffic fatalities, campus shootings, and cancer as mismanagement. I wonder why tornadoes seem more inclined to rip off the roofs in poor neighborhoods as opposed to wealthy ones. I'm shocked when I hear that more adults and children are currently victims of human trafficking than the total number of people victimized by the African slave trade during the sixteenth and seventeenth centuries. There's genocide in Darfur and daily suicide bombings in the Middle East. Am I not supposed to question management of any of that?

JUSTICE AND JUSTUS

But forget for a minute about world-shaking current events. Forget about life-and-death issues. Many—maybe most—of the troubles that suck us spiritually dry happen on a much smaller scale. They are minor setbacks; little disappointments. Nobody's going to die, but that doesn't mean the hits don't hurt and bruise. I've often wondered what it would have been like to be Justus, the almost apostle.

Soon after the resurrection of Jesus and his subsequent ascension back to heaven (Acts 1:1–11) the disciples returned to Jerusalem. You'll recall that after Judas's guilt-ridden suicide there was a vacancy in the dozen. Peter told the assembly that it was time to select a suitable replacement for Judas. He declared it was "necessary to choose one of the men who have been with us the whole time the Lord Jesus went in and out among us, beginning from John's baptism to the time when Jesus was taken up from us. For one of these must become a witness with us of his resurrection" (Acts 1:21–22).

The assembly proposed two men as qualified candidates: Joseph (also called Justus) and Matthias. If this episode had taken place in twenty-first-century America, it is likely that the duo would have embarked upon well-funded, mudslinging campaigns or starred on a reality TV show like *The Apprentice*, where a religious Donald Trump figure would have fired the loser in the final episode. But in this instance, not even super delegates were appointed. Instead, they voiced a prayer: "Lord, you know everyone's heart. Show us which of these two you have chosen to take over this apostolic ministry..." (Acts 1:24–25). Then they cast lots, which is another way of saying they rolled dice, flipped a coin, or drew straws. The winning number belonged to Matthias, and he was appointed to join the eleven other apostles.

There was no indication that Justus asked for a recount or a best of three. Luke, the writer of the account (Acts 1:12–26), doesn't tell us how either of the candidates responded to the results. One is left to assume that Matthias did not take on a prominent role in his new assignment to the apostolic team. His name is not mentioned again in the book of Acts, which gives a condensed history of the activities and spread of the early church. Neither is he mentioned in the subsequent writings of other New Testament authors like Paul, Peter, or James. That's not to say that Matthias didn't do important work of eternal significance. We just don't have any record of his deeds after his appointment.

But Justus is the guy I've always wondered about. How did he react when he wasn't chosen? My imagination goes to the coronation ceremony of beauty pageants. The climactic scene is always the same. Two contestants remain, but only one will be crowned Miss America, while the other beauty is given the consolation prize of first runner-up. The new queen is obliged to break into tears while the runner-up must congratulate her before slipping into the background with the other also-rans. The audience is reminded that should the winner be unable to fulfill her role (or get disqualified for risqué photos on the Internet) then the first runner-up would snatch the crown for the duration of the reign. You have to wonder how many women in that position have secretly fantasized about reprising a Tanya Harding-Nancy Kerrigan mugging.

How did Justus respond outwardly when Matthias won the coin toss? How did he respond inwardly? Was he disappointed? Was he relieved?

(After all, the job would entail a lot of travel.) Justus couldn't take a coin flip as a personal rejection of his character and abilities, or could he?

> Regardless of what happens, we're called to be faithful. Regardless of what happens, God loves us. Regardless of what happens, God has a plan, and it's a good one.

They all believed that God was the one who controlled the flip. What if he believed himself to be the better qualified man? In the same vein, I've often wondered what it was like for Al Gore in 2000 when he won the popular vote, and the electoral vote was so close that the disputed hanging chads of Florida had to visit the Supreme Court. No candidate had ever lost a presidential election by a closer margin than Gore did to George W. Bush. Recall that as the sitting Vice President of the United States at the time of the election, Gore was already a White House resident. When the Supreme Court declared Bush the winner, Gore was suddenly out of a job and had to evacuate the West Wing. After the moving truck left Washington for their home state of Tennessee, Al and Tipper Gore followed in a rented Ford Taurus.

How did a man respond when he was just a few dimpled chads away from the most powerful office on the planet? How did an ancient man react when he was moments away from being on the inner circle of the most phenomenal religious movement the world would ever know? What has always struck me most is that immediately following Matthias's promotion, Justus likely resumed his regular job and standard routine amidst his existing relationships in a familiar community. Nothing really changed for Justus. But here's the kicker: God expected the same level of faithfulness from Justus as a returning tradesman that he would have expected from him as an apostle. If God gave Justus time to pout, he would not have given him long to do so. My point is that even when something undesirable happens, there is always a "regardless of what happens" that hovers over all. Regardless of what happens, we're called to be faithful. Regardless of what happens, God loves us. Regardless of what happens, God has a plan, and it's a good one.

Then there are times that the disappointment or anguish is over something desired or desirable that does *not* happen—a job doesn't materialize, a promotion goes to someone else, a coveted spot on the team is filled by another player, a proposal is declined, a manuscript is rejected, an acceptance letter goes to another applicant, a house still won't sell, a marriage proposal never comes, a plea for a second chance is rebuffed, or a prayer for healing isn't answered. It is at these times that we, like Justus, must strive to live extraordinary lives above the ground level of our disappointment or grief. Maybe you've been a victim of an emotional tornado. That doesn't mean God invites you to live the rest of your life in the emotional equivalent of an underground storm shelter. Neither is it okay to make others around you miserable—especially those you live with—because of the toxic bitterness you feel entitled to.

I'm amazed, inspired, and challenged by the response of my friend, Veronica, to cancer. In addition to her refusal to remain homebound, quit work, wear "sick clothes," or marinate in self-pity, Veronica told me that she decided early on that "feeling like crap doesn't give me permission to be rude to my family." That statement stung me. I readily give myself permission to be cranky and short tempered on a bad day, when my bad days are ten times better than Veronica's good days.

For me the "whatever happens" mandate is tethered to a necessary belief that we can trust Paul's word to the church in Rome: "We know that in all things God works for the good of those who love him, who have been called according to his purpose" (Romans 8:28). Can you make the connection between "in all things" and "whatever happens"? This response to Romans 8:28 is deeper than just throwing up our hands and saying, "Well, everything happens for a reason." I once overheard a visitor say that to a set of demolished parents in a pediatric intensive care unit waiting room, and I wanted to go over and slap the guy! And that was before he said, "Maybe God needs another little angel in heaven." At that point I was grinding my teeth right through the enamel. I wanted

> God is able to work in the midst of all things and often in spite of all things. He desires to join us in bringing something redemptive out of the crisis.

to tell the guy to get lost, tell the couple to ignore what he said because he was not speaking for God, and remind them that Jesus never told the bereaved parent of an only son, "Well, everything happens for a reason." Jesus was regularly moved to compassion and was fully engaged with the afflicted and the oppressed. Jesus did not sprinkle devastated people with trite clichés. He was the image of his Father, showing us what the love of God really looks like.

With that being said, how are we to engage with the statement, "in all things God works for the good"? Is that just supposed to be our fallback consolation after we have finally climbed out of the pit of grieving? Is that what is really waiting for us once God thinks we can handle it? What is "the good" for someone who is left to excavate themselves from a divorce, sexual abuse, bankruptcy because of a dishonest business partner, a son's drug addiction, or the permanent birth defect of a long-awaited baby? What pearls are we to find in the oysters of the abduction of a child, the terminal cancer of a single mom, a parent's alcoholism, or a brother's suicide?

> The world is broken by sin. We are all going to experience brokenness. The question is how we will respond to brokenness.

God is able to work in the midst of all things and often in spite of all things. He desires to join us in bringing something redemptive out of the crisis. Our pain and loss need not be the end of the story or what defines us. The world is broken by sin. We are all going to experience brokenness. The question is how we will respond to brokenness. Will we respond in a way that grows us and brings blessing to others? Private tragedy has birthed much of the social activism and personal ministry that makes a profound difference in our communities and our world. Julie Taylor, whose son Tim was killed by a drunk driver, was so hurt and angered by her own experience that she founded Mothers Against Drunk Driving (MADD). That organization has impacted DUI laws, alcohol advertising, bars' and bartenders' responsibility for patron intoxication, driver's education curriculum, and even the free taxi rides offered on New Year's Eve by many cities.

Steve Grissom channeled the painful experience of his own divorce into a nationwide ministry of resources and

> I'll be the first to admit that if God is going to work everything out for good, I would much prefer that he allow me to define what we mean by "good."

support groups called DivorceCare. On a smaller scale my friends in South Carolina, Eddie and Gail Turner, have a local ministry to those grieving the death of a loved one. As a young bride, Gail's first husband was killed in an auto accident. Eddie's twenty-year-old son was murdered. Together they have chosen to harness and burn their pain as fuel for something redemptive and helpful to others, which in turn spurs their own healing.

I have witnessed it over and over: people's greatest ministry is often built on the platform of their greatest brokenness. They are living examples of what Paul wrote in 2 Corinthians 1:3-4: "...the Father of compassion and the God of all comfort, who comforts us in all our troubles, so that we can comfort those in any trouble with the comfort we ourselves have received from God." It's vital that we not waste our pain but recycle and redeem it.

Part of the difficulty of embracing the reassuring truth of Romans 8 is the wide gap between God's idea of what is good and beneficial and ours. I'll be the first to admit that if God is going to work everything out for good, I would much prefer that he allow me to define what we mean by "good." I'm really clear on what I think good results and outcomes would be, and they don't always match up with what I experience. But Romans 8:29 gives us a partial glimpse into how God defines the ultimate good mentioned in verse 28: "For those God foreknew he also predestined to become conformed to the likeness of His Son." From God's perspective, what's really good for us is the transformation of our character. Let's be honest—is that your highest goal? Maybe it's my goal in my better moments. But day in and day out, I've usually got my mind on other things.

As much as we wish God would transfer his focus to more external and circumstantial matters, such as restored health, mortgage payments, and career transitions, God is primarily interested in pulling off an inside job. God is certainly at work all around us, but his primary transforming work is aimed at our minds and hearts. That was illustrated in the ministry and message of Jesus. Despite the pressures to be a political rebel and social system reformer, he was least interested in overthrowing Roman rule and most interested in drilling down to the core determinant of all social systems—the emotional and spiritual heart of the individual.

*   *   *

In the feel-good film *The Karate Kid*, after seeing his young neighbor bullied, Mr. Miyagi agrees to mentor the young Daniel and teach him karate. While the student eagerly awaits his first lesson, Mr. Miyagi keeps putting the boy to work around his house—painting his fence, sanding his wooden deck floors, and waxing his cars. Daniel's confusion turns to irritation and then he explodes in anger as he accuses his mentor of wasting his time and even using him for free manual labor. As Daniel curses and walks away, Miyagi calls him back and orders him to repeat the movements of "paint the fence," "sand the floor," and "wax on/wax off." In a moment of revelation as Miyagi attacks, Daniel learns that those three now well-conditioned movements, motions that comprised what he thought to be meaningless work, had actually become the fluid foundations of his training in karate. What Daniel thought to be manipulation was in fact preparation.

This scene wonderfully illustrates how God is often working in me and around me in ways that leave me failing to comprehend their meaning or purpose. I'm prone to think that God is not doing anything, or that he is jerking me around, when in fact he is preparing me for an upcoming life experience or an assignment.

Sometimes I remind myself of King George of England's journal entry recorded July 4, 1776. On that day in Philadelphia, America's Founding Fathers were signing the Declaration of Independence. An ocean away, the king wrote succinctly: "Nothing of significance occurred today." Could the British monarch have been more wrong? Far beyond his awareness, something of profound import was happening. But the king could only see

> I'm prone to think that God is not doing anything, or that he is jerking me around, when in fact he is preparing me for an upcoming life experience or an assignment.

the act of the play that was taking place on the stage in front of him. Much was happening offstage and out of the spotlight. Something very significant was set in motion that day. He would learn of it and be disturbed by it soon enough.

Long before King George, while the world was preoccupied with its business—trekking home for the census, keeping watch over their flocks by night, tending to their inns—a frightened teenage mother gave birth to a baby boy and placed him in a feeding trough for lack of a proper bed. And that baby turned out to be the Savior of the world. There is more happening in your life than you know. God is working behind the scenes and beyond your awareness. There are strategic things set in motion on your behalf that are still hidden and unknown to you. So when you're thinking that life sucks because nothing is happening or nothing is changing, check the calendar—it may be July 4, 1776 in your world.

7

Moving from Why?
to What Next?

My parents' generation remembers exactly where they were when they heard that President Kennedy had been shot. Their parents recall where they were and exactly what they were doing when they got news that Pearl Harbor had been bombed. For my generation it was September 11. All of us recall where we were, what we were doing, and how we found out about the terrorists crashing planes in New York City, Washington D.C., and Pennsylvania.

We can remember the first images of the burning towers we saw on the television, then the report and video of the fiery crash into the Pentagon. We watched the unthinkable in shock and disbelief. "This can't really be happening. Not here." We huddled, we held hands, we wept, and we made phone calls. For days we couldn't stop watching the news. Who knows how many times we saw the video clip of that second plane smashing into the north tower. We watched the news at night as rescue teams sifted through the rubble.

Early in the morning of 9/11 I was on a park bench across the street from the church, sipping Dunkin' Donuts' coffee and writing in my journal. It was going to be a beautiful Tuesday. I was at such peace on this particular morning that I was inclined to write on nothing more profound than my observation of an inchworm's movements on a nearby tree trunk.

> The caterpillar working its way up the tree doesn't crawl; he pushes off from his hindquarters and creates a wave that carries his tiny appendages forward as its back arcs. He moves by riding his own wave.

I didn't have a cell phone or a beeper at the time, so no one was trying to reach me.

I concluded my lighthearted meditation and headed over to the church, ready to take on the day from a place of peace. Strolling into the office, I first encountered the receptionist. Her eyes were red and watery. She had the radio on, and I could hear that it was news, not music. She looked up and her voice broke, "Everyone is in Stephen's office." Stephen's office was close by, but it was enough steps away that my imagination had time to ricochet off a number of possibilities. Indeed, everyone was in Stephen's office, silent and all facing the same direction, staring at a small TV.

The second tower had already been hit, which confirmed suspicions that the first hit was no accident. The images were so disturbing. Then the images and story of New York City yielded to the live footage of another crash scene at the Pentagon. What was happening? What would be next? We watched the TV all morning. I slipped out just long enough to call home and tell Dorrie to turn on the TV. That's all I said. It was all I knew to say. We all watched as the first tower began to crumble and disintegrate right before our eyes. There were few words expressed—just gasps, sighs, and sniffles. The broadcasters were echoing our thoughts and questions. We knew there were people inside—office workers, policemen, firemen, and rescue workers. They couldn't know the tower would begin to collapse in on itself. Nobody knew. We didn't think that the carnage of the towers could get any worse unless they were hit by more planes. The image of that smoldering tower imploding within seconds is forever etched into our brains. Then the second tower mimicked the first one.

This must have been what someone meant when they coined the phrase "all hell breaking loose." This was hell taking possession of earthly ground. In the midst of shock and mourning we had enough clarity of thought to know that the world as we knew it was instantly forever changed. We didn't know exactly how it would be different; we just knew that a turning point had occurred. Days later I returned to the park and wrote in my journal. There was no inchworm in this entry, just uncertainty, some fear, and maybe the unspoken question, *why.*

This week the world changed. The future will reveal to what extent, but it's now forever different. One journalist referred to Monday, the day before 9/11, as "the world as we knew it." The trees around me in this park look the same, but they are rooted now in the soil of an altered world; they tower in the air of a different nation.

THE OTHER FALLEN TOWER

In the time of Jesus' ministry a well-known tower in Jerusalem fell. It wasn't an act of terrorism, just a freak accident. The tower's collapse didn't result in the loss of thousands of lives; just eighteen. But in a city like Jerusalem, just as in your town, the sudden and tragic death of eighteen people would be front-page news. And if any of your loved ones had been among the dead, the total number of victims would be a secondary concern. Regardless, eighteen killed is eighteen too many.

Though the tower's fall was not an act of terrorism or personal evil, the people of Jerusalem were well acquainted with another incident of brutal violence that made them shudder. It seems that Pilate—surely the same Pilate who presided over Jesus' crucifixion—murdered a group of Galileans, mixing their blood with their sacrifices. The slaughter must have happened while the Galileans were worshiping (hence the detail that their blood mixed with their sacrifices), but the clues are scanty. The only reference to the incident is a brief mention in Luke 13:1: "Now there were some present at that time who told Jesus about the Galileans whose blood Pilate had mixed with their sacrifices."

> Why did this happen? Why did God allow it to happen? Why were good people caused to suffer at the hands of an evil man? Their *why* questions were like splinters driven so deeply into the flesh they could not remove them.

The passage doesn't say why the people mentioned this incident to Jesus. It doesn't mention that they asked him any questions. On the surface, they were just giving a report. But Jesus had a habit of drilling through the surface to the underlying question. And the question here was *why*. Why did this happen? Why did God allow it to happen? Why were good people caused to suffer at the hands of an evil man? Their *why* questions were like splinters driven so deeply into the flesh they could not remove them. No tip to grasp and tug, each splinter was entirely lodged beneath the surface of the skin. The pain reminded them of its presence. Maybe Jesus could make some sense of the senseless. Maybe he could remove the splinter.

So Jesus tackled the *why* question—not by making things simpler, but by making them more complicated. The people brought up the issue of human evil—man's inhumanity to man. Next to that thorny issue, Jesus placed a second thorny issue: the seemingly random suffering caused by the collapse of the tower in Siloam. Then he placed himself right in the middle of the thorns.

LUKE 13:1–5

Jesus answered, "Do you think that these Galileans were worse sinners than all the other Galileans because they suffered this way? I tell you, no! But unless you repent, you too will all perish. Or those eighteen who died when the tower in Siloam fell on them—do you think they were more guilty than all the others living in Jerusalem? I tell you, no! But unless you repent, you too will all perish." (Luke 13:2–5)

Why? It's a perfectly natural question. We humans feel compelled to make sense out of our world. We don't deal well with ambiguity. We want clarity. We want answers. Mysteries make for best-selling novels— as long as they're solved at the end.

Actually, many of the Jews of Jesus' day did have an explanation that cleaned up messy dilemmas like Pilate's slaughter and the tower's fall. Bad things don't happen to good people, went the argument; instead, they happen to people who only appeared good, but in fact were secretly sinful and thus judged for their wickedness. In this way, God takes extreme measures to punish and weed out hypocrites. Let it be a lesson to you all that God knows your secret sin and you might end up on the bad end of a blood letting. Thus one of the prevailing explanations for suffering was reduced to something quite simplistic and judgmental. It was also useful for "putting the fear of God in you" in order to get greater compliance to the moral code.

One of the reasons we may seek a second medical opinion is that we desire another perspective from an authoritative source. We're even more likely to seek out that alternative perspective if we don't like the first one, perhaps due to a dark diagnosis or a gloomy prognosis, or maybe the suggestion of extensive or radical treatment. We hope the second doctor has better news. The original diagnosis that the people of Jesus' day had grown up with was that bad things happen to bad people, which undoubtedly created confusion when terrible things regularly befell good and innocent people.

Jesus offered his perspective to help them with theirs. It is not known how his audience responded to it. To one the truth may be good news; to another the same truth is unacceptable or unwelcome. If beauty is in the eye of the beholder, then good news resides in the perspective of the recipient. Jesus would tell them the truth. He refuted their solution of the mystery but did not offer his own tidy solution to the agonizing question of why there is so much suffering in the world. But, oh, how we want him to answer it! We want him to say, "Here's why the Galileans died, and here's why eighteen were crushed to death in Jerusalem…" We want him to explain why thousands are killed in earthquakes and cyclones and why teenagers are gunned down in schools. We demand to know why single parents get cancer and why innocent children are brutally abused. Luke 13 would seem the perfect setting for Jesus to field the question and answer it to our great satisfaction, and thus relieve some of the stress of our suffering. He declined. So did the angel before Gideon. So did God in response to Job.

The passage actually makes a distinction between two dynamics of human suffering: evil and affliction. Evil is what we suffer at the hands of another, while affliction comes in ways that were not schemed or inflicted by others. For example, the martyrdom of the Galileans was an evil act. Suffering touched by evil includes such things as abuse, assault, murder, and rape. Affliction includes such things as injuries or death caused by natural disasters, famines, or accidents, as well as illnesses and diseases. Thus far we have defined suffering as something that is done to our bodies, but of course we may experience evil and affliction in other ways that are just as damaging. We may be robbed by a gunman

> Jesus acknowledges these two distinct sources of suffering, but he draws a similar conclusion to each—that life's most tragic experience is not human suffering and victimization. Rather, it is perishing and facing eternity without God.

or bankrupted by a dishonest business partner. Our suffering may come from the intentional emotional abuse of a parent or through the loneliness of an unwanted divorce.

Jesus acknowledges these two distinct sources of suffering, but he draws a similar conclusion to each—that life's most tragic experience is not human suffering and victimization. Rather, it is perishing and facing eternity without God. Jesus implies that we aren't likely to choose how, when, or where we will die. Indeed, the circumstances surrounding our death may be tragic, but we can choose to repent.

Repentance is not a popular word. It doesn't just sound old school, it sounds archaic and out of touch. Repent. It conjures up a "turn or burn" preacher on a sawdust floor or on a street corner screaming about the coming wrath of God. "Jesus is coming back soon and he's ticked off! Repent of your evil ways so that you can escape the flames even now licking at the soles of your Reeboks!"

> Repentance is not a popular word. It doesn't just sound old school, it sounds archaic and out of touch.

The word *repent* simply means to stop, turn, and go in a much different direction. It means to make a change. When I founded LifeChange Counseling Services I inserted a U-turn arrow inside the *C* to emphasize the dynamics and hope of true change. I begin with the assumption that people come to me for counseling because there is something they want to change. People who feel that their life is running smoothly, their emotions are manageable, and their relationships are free of conflict do not call me to schedule appointments. People call me when there is a need for understanding, healing, recovery, repair, rebuilding, transition, progress, deliverance, victory, restoration, reconciliation, or breakthrough. In other words, change. People come to me because there is something they want to see changed. Most are not coming in need of repentance in the traditional impression of the word, meaning they need to confess and cease committing some sin.

> It's not wrong to ask *why*, but don't stake your happiness or your faithfulness on getting a satisfactory answer. Throughout the Gospels, Jesus shifts the question from *why* to *what next.*

Rather, most are in need of a wise and caring tour guide for the life-change journey they are on. I consider it an honor and a privilege to be invited to join my clients for a brief time on their way.

It's not wrong to ask *why*, but don't stake your happiness or your faithfulness on getting a satisfactory answer. Throughout the Gospels, Jesus shifts the question from *why* to *what next.* The people's implied question is both past tense (why did that happen?) and pointed outward, away from the speaker (why did that happen to them?). Jesus asks a more immediate and personal question: How are you going to live now?

We see a somewhat similar theme in Jesus' response to another *why* question, this one posed by his own disciples. Upon encountering a man born blind, they wanted to know where to lay the fault. "Rabbi," they asked Jesus, "who sinned, this man or his parents, that he was born blind?" (John 9:2). The assumption is that there is indeed someone to blame. However, when bad things happen or tragedy strikes, does it really help us feel better, ease the pain, and aid our recovery to track down someone to blame?

But I'm inclined to cut the disciples some slack and give them credit for recognizing the moral, logical, and theological dilemma in front of them. "Rabbi, we've been taught that when someone has a disease it is because either he has sinned or, if he is young, his parents committed some terrible sin. But this man was born blind so he could not have sinned in the womb, right? So was the baby punished with blindness because his parents sinned? That doesn't seem quite fair. Why not strike one or both of the parents blind?" The disciples encounter a living dilemma that begs for an explanation, and they're questioning both of the traditional rationales given to resolve it.

You can see the wheels turning in the minds of the disciples as they encounter the blind man. "Rabbi, which of the two explanations applies to this case? Neither one makes good sense to us but you're smarter and wiser than us, so which is it? Are the parents to blame or was it the kid?" "Neither," Jesus responds. You can just see the perplexed disciples' confusion going up a notch. "Neither?" "Right. Neither this man nor his parents sinned," said Jesus. Then he adds, "This happened so that the work of God might be displayed in his life."

Jesus is saying, "Forget about who is to blame. There are much more interesting and significant things at stake here." The primary thing at stake is the power of God to transform a terrible situation and make something good out of it. The blind man's darkness became a conduit for the light of God in that man's life, in the lives of those who witnessed his healing, and in millions of lives in the two thousand years since. Jesus overruled the man's blindness just as he ultimately overrules every hardship and sadness.

Jesus' next words shine on it the light of elaboration. "As long as it is day, we must do the work of him who sent me. Night is coming, when no one can work. While I am in the world, I am the light of the world" (John 9:4–5). He is saying, "You've seen what I can do. Now, what are you going to do about it?" Jesus denies the simple, linear thinking that seeks an easy cause-and-effect answer to a dilemma. Then Jesus asserts himself to change the question *why did this happen?* to *what should we do now?* Although Jesus certainly understands our agonizing *why* questions, apparently he finds little point in his or our camping out in explanations of past events. Instead, he moves the disciples from *why* to *what now*. He directs them from a question that focuses on the past to one that focuses on the present. Jesus addresses the *what now* issue by saying, "As long as it is day, we must do the work of God." In other words, instead of obsessing over past causation, Jesus redirects us to attend to the only place we can live and intervene—the present. The present is the only point on the time continuum where choices and decisions can be made and where action is taken. In his outstanding book, *Ruthless Trust*, author Brennan Manning connects this action to faith saying, "It is an act of radical trust that God can be encountered at no other time and in no other place than the present moment."[11]

Jesus does something in John 9 that he also does in Luke 13. He not only changes the focus from past causation to present action, but he redirects the spotlight from landing on others to finding us. In John 9 Jesus changes the question from just being about the blind man to being about himself and his disciples. Likewise, instead of focusing on the tortured Galileans and tower victims featured on the stage of the discussion, Jesus reveals that the real drama resides with the audience, and that the most pertinent question is one that the listener must answer for himself. Jesus sidesteps the *why* questions in Luke 13 and John 9 because he wants to redirect his listeners to the more pertinent *what now* question. While I am proposing that Jesus does not directly answer, why did this happen? I should pause to acknowledge that there are two other possible explanations for Jesus not answering *why*.

One explanation says that Jesus doesn't know the answer. Perhaps he has no insider information on the real causes of the specific incidents of evil and suffering. Perhaps he is as baffled by the dilemma as his listeners and his disciples. This explanation reduces Jesus to something like a coy politician who avoids a hard question during a debate and crafts a verbal smokescreen to hide his ignorance. If Jesus doesn't know, then he should just say so. But Jesus is not a slippery politician. He is not expertly disguising his knowledge gap so as not to undermine the confidence of his followers.

A second explanation holds that Jesus indeed knows the answers, knows the behind-the-scenes scoop, but determines that we can't comprehend or handle the info. The first implies that we are something like first graders unable to grasp the complexities of trigonometry. The second invokes memories of the exchange between Tom Cruise and Jack Nicholson in a climatic scene from *A Few Good Men*.

CRUISE. I want the truth!
NICHOLSON. You can't handle the truth!

This is akin to a defiant God saying, "You think you want to know why, but you really don't because you'd find the truth too disturbing. Your little peon brain and heart couldn't handle it."

At this very moment my ten-year-old car is in the shop for extensive and expensive engine and transmission repairs. I love cars, but I'm not very mechanical. It's all I can do to check (not change) my own oil and keep the tires inflated. So when a knowledgeable mechanic starts explaining exactly why the EGR valve is sending a bad code to the Power Control Module, he loses me pretty quickly. You can probably guess what I want to know. How much is it going to cost to fix it? My bottom line inquiry is not really how transmissions go bad or how mine broke, but what do we do about it now? Can it be fixed, how long will it take, and how much will it cost? My questions are less *why* and more *now what*. When talking to a layperson, a wise expert gives brief explanations with just enough details to aid in making a decision. That approach is not condescending; it is courteous. God is not condescending. Yes, he knows that "we now see through a glass dimly," but he doesn't treat us as though we have only slightly more intelligence and understanding than sea plankton. He gives us scanty details because he recognizes what we really need to keep moving forward.

In my counseling practice I often encounter people who go to the mat with God over the *why* question. I never refute their need to ask and seek answers. In their acute pain they are dusting for cosmic clues at the scene of what feels like a spiritual crime. God is big and secure; he doesn't need me to shield him from broken people who want to pound on his chest. God has never asked me to take on the role of a Secret Service agent and protect him from would-be attackers. But at some point in the grief recovery process, when I feel the timing is right, I introduce my clients to a new and important truth—the *what now* question. It is a gradual transition and not a smooth one; it is marked by progress and setbacks. I never try to move a grieving person to get over a profound loss. We're not talking about getting over a momentary virus like the flu. This is the permanent loss of someone deeply loved or the loss of something highly valued.

> But at some point in the grief recovery process, when I feel the timing is right, I introduce my clients to a new and important truth—the *what now* question.

Gerald Sittser, author of *A Grace Disguised: How the Soul Grows through Loss*, was driving the family van back from a local mission project when his vehicle was struck by a drunken driver. Gerald was the sole surviving passenger. His wife, mother, and daughter were instantly killed. In his refreshingly honest book describing his journey of healing and recovery, Sittser describes a transformation brought about by grieving: "I did not get over the loss of my loved ones; rather, I absorbed the loss into my life, like soil receives decaying matter, until it became part of who I am."[12] Sittser discovered that healthy recovery and healing from grief finds a way to integrate the past into the present and future. The expectation that we "get over" or "move on" from a profound loss or crisis is not only unrealistic, but it may even be harmful in its call to amputate grief rather than integrate it into a new way of living.

8

Content or Discontent: Choosing My Tent

Discontent is a joy stealer. You would think Hollywood celebrities would be content with fame, attention, money, and dazzling spouses. If so, then why do they pile up divorces as if they had a buy-five-get-one-free card?

In his letter to the Philippians the apostle Paul has something important to say about contentment. Like composting and reframing, growing in contentment is a vigorous exercise in perspective. Paul exhorts us to get to the gym. Contentment is elusive, isn't it? Contentment is like that mechanical rabbit that runs around the inner ring at the greyhound race track. The dogs never catch it. If one of the greyhounds ever finds out that the bunny isn't real and tells the other dogs...

Fill in the blanks below faintly with a pencil. Be honest and write the first response that comes to mind:

- Life is going to be really good when_____
  _____.
- Life would be great if only_____
  _____.
- I know I'd be happier if I had_____
  _____.
- Life was really good back when_____
  _____.

There are often wonderful things about the past that we miss, and there are exciting possibilities in the future that we long for. Yet it is possible to get stuck lamenting over what is no more, wanting what might be, or resenting what may never be. Discontentment holds today's joy hostage with a list of demands of how things should be.

> Discontentment holds today's joy hostage with a list of demands of how things should be.

Have you ever looked around at what was happening in your life and said, "How did I get here? This isn't where I wanted to be. This isn't what I planned for." Once while driving from West Palm Beach to Orlando on Florida's Turnpike, I stopped at one of the rest areas for a snack. I put my coins in one of those vending machines with the letter-number combinations and punched R-7 for a Snickers bar. The machine hummed and the corkscrew turned in the top left-hand corner and a bag of barbecue pork rinds jumped off instead. In my most ravenous hunger I would never choose barbecue pork rinds. Let's just say I was less than content with what I got for my investment. Some of you feel like that too. I wanted filet mignon and got Spam instead. I've worked hard, I've been faithful, and I've hoped, prayed, and waited for X, but got Y.

When my son Trevor was four years old, one evening he came downstairs into the living room around 9 p.m., while we were watching television after putting him to bed. "Trevor, what are you doing out of bed?" I asked. With a sheepish look on his face and in a less than convincing tone he said, "I was having a bad dream." "Well then," I responded insightfully, "you're awake now, so the nightmare must be over." Trevor replied with a suppressed grin, "No Dad, I'm still having it."

Some of you may feel like you're not waking up from your nightmare. If you find contentment elusive, if you struggle with unfulfilled expectations, then pull your chair up close and reflect on Paul's words to the Philippians.

> I rejoice greatly in the Lord that at last you have renewed your concern for me. Indeed, you have been concerned, but you had no opportunity to show it. I am not saying this because I am in need, for I have learned to be content whatever the circumstances. I know what it is to be in need, and I know what it is to have plenty. I have learned the secret of being content in any and every situation, whether well fed or hungry, whether living in plenty or in want. I can do everything through him who gives me strength. (Philippians 4:10–13)

I'm sure I don't have to remind you, Paul was imprisoned when he wrote those words. Paul learned to be content whatever the circumstances. Have you? I'm still working on that one myself.

Paul is a worthy mentor on contentment because he understands unfulfilled expectations. Instead of relishing the freedom to preach outside on Roman streets and in courtyards to the curious, the receptive, and the skeptical, Paul sees little light at all during his day. He can walk no further than his house arrest allows. His companionship is a shift of prison guards, and perhaps Timothy or Epaphroditus on occasion. This isn't the screenplay he wrote. No one seems to be on cue. No one is reading their lines correctly.

WHAT CONTENTMENT IS AND IS NOT

Before we say what contentment is, let's clear up two misconceptions.

Contentment Is Not Complacency

Contentment does not mean that we don't pursue goals or work for change. To have a vision means to be able to see and describe a preferable future. Even prayer itself is the expression of a holy discontent with the status quo. Contentment does not mean that you don't have a preference—if you had given Paul the option of staying in jail or getting out, what do you think he would have chosen? God is not asking you to neuter all your preferences. "Not my will but yours be done" does not mean that you are immobilized into inactivity, forsaking all proactive behavior. I'll have more to say about this in the final chapter, "God Still Invites You to Dream Big." For now just understand that contentment does not mean that you bury your dreams in an unmarked grave, or that you contort your hopes into some posture of indifference.

Contentment Allows for Disappointment

Paul writes in 2 Corinthians 4:8, "We are pressed on every side by troubles but not crushed and broken. We are perplexed because we don't know why things happen as they do, but we don't give up and quit" (TLB). Do you see it? We're perplexed but not in despair. This isn't perplexed as in "I know I left those keys around here somewhere." This is being perplexed by a hard and confusing reality. It is feeling truly disappointed.

Not long after we moved to Tennessee, I found out that we had received a good offer on our house in Greenville, South Carolina. It was cause for celebration; the house hadn't been on the market long at all. We wouldn't be making double house payments after all. Our exhilaration was short-lived though. Within twenty-four hours we got another call; our buyer's offer had fallen through. My shoulders slumped, my spirit sunk, and I was in a useless funk for the rest of the day and most of the next. I was sorely disappointed. It felt like a cruel game of now you see it, now you don't. I would have preferred to have never gotten the offer in the first place instead of getting one and having it collapse. I sulked for a while before I regained some energy and perspective.

It was six more months before the house sold. It was painful to pay the mortgage every month on a house that my family was not living in. It was not only terribly costly but it felt like such a waste, like running twelve hundred dollars through the paper shredder on the fifteenth of every month. "God, I know you don't want us to waste money, so I know you want our house to sell soon. Don't you?" I remember Calvin Miller writing about the time that his neighbor's house sold in three days while his own house stayed on the market for a year. During that year he reminded God of his sacrificial ministry as a pastor compared to the neighbor who seemingly did little to justify such favor. Miller reminded God that his house was the host site for many Bible studies and prayer meetings. And in case God forgot, Miller helped God recall his faithfulness in tithing and charitable giving. It seemed so unfair, as if the undeserving neighbor had broken in line in front of him. Calvin Miller's breakthrough revelation was that he had been worshiping "the God of the Good Deal." He realized that he was counting on his own faithfulness and obedience to give him favored status for the things he wanted.[13]

Contentment in a situation does not mean that we are not disappointed or that we never grieve. Contentment, however, does mean that we are not immobilized by despair when life strays from the script we wrote for it. Or maybe we find ourselves stuck in despair for a season, but we do not take up permanent residence there. It is important to get a handle on discontentment because the potential reactions to it include not only despair, but also anger, blame, resentment, rebellion, and addictive behaviors (eating, gambling, pornography, and shopping).

THREE COMPARISON TRAPS

In my own life and in counseling others, I have discovered that there are three "comparison traps" that are guaranteed to set us up for discontentment. Animals caught in hunters' traps have been known to chew off a leg to free themselves from the capture and the pain of a steel-jawed trap. It's better to avoid these traps than be forced to gnaw your leg off!

> Watch out for words like *should* or *deserve.*

Comparison Trap #1: *What I Have Now vs. What I Should Have*
This comparison obsesses about what I want, need, or think I deserve. Calvin Miller put it this way: "When we focus on how things ought to be, the *oughtness* can be so consuming it steals our peace...We are uncomfortable with the moment. We live well for how things ought to be but not so well with how things are. The whole key to living in happiness is our ability to disentangle ourselves from *oughtness* until we have peace with *isness.*"[14]

Watch out for words like *should* or *deserve.* Those words are often rooted in expectations that one or more of the following be recognized and rewarded by God and/or another person:

- My hard work
- My faithfulness
- My longevity
- My character
- My perseverance
- My patience
- My ability, skill, or talent
- My experience
- My righteousness
- My giving up vacation time to go on a mission trip

- My sacrificial giving and/or tithe
- My compassion
- Other:_____

Not having what we want or what we think we need tends to promote discontent. Not having what we feel we rightly deserve not only leads to discontent but branches out into resentment.

I'm vulnerable to discontentment because of what I think should happen in this season of my life. I should be consistently and reliably providing for the financial security of my family through my therapy practice. That's not a wild and far out should, but it is one that can trap me into discontentment and ultimately despair, which does nothing to spur me on to do the work necessary to improve our lot. Self-pity does not provoke my creativity, increase my marketing efforts, or improve my networking skills. Self-pity is a slow leak through which peace and joy escape. While immobilized on the roadside like a stranded motorist, possibilities for change and opportunities for improvement pass me by.

Comparison Trap #2: What I Have Now vs. What I Once Had
Paul had known status, wealth, and comfort as a Pharisee in the Hebrew culture. He did not whine about his present condition in contrast to his pre-conversion life of ease or his life of ministry prior to being jailed. We all face losses. We should grieve them, but camping out in the past and dwelling on what we once had will sabotage contentment.

I do want to add a qualifier here. I do not want to be guilty of minimizing profound loss or judging a legitimate and necessary grief. Some of you have lost the following:

- A close family member or friend to an unexpected death
- A spouse and a way life as you knew it because of divorce
- A fiancé/fiancée because of a broken engagement
- Your health

- A beloved home because of foreclosure, a storm, or relocation
- Your job
- A significant percentage of your savings
- Other:_____

_____

It is imperative to acknowledge and grieve your losses. Sometimes others will seem to imply that you should be over the loss by now and be done with your grieving. "Put on a happy face and come to the party," they'll say.

I'm not willing to set boundaries on grief or offer formulas for recovery. There is not enough space here to do justice to an issue addressed in entire volumes. I will say that grieving should not be done alone, and I recommend you seek a wise Christian counselor or therapist who can compassionately walk with you and escort you through the maze of grief. Whatever our loss

> Whatever our loss and however deep our grief, eventually we come to some kind of crossroads that requires us to make a tough decision.

and however deep our grief, eventually we come to some kind of cross-roads that requires us to make a tough decision. While not denying my hurt or thinking that I must somehow simply get over it, I nevertheless face a choice. I can erect a monument here in the place of loss and grief and say, "This is where my life stopped and will permanently be buried." Or, I can erect a marker and say, "This is where my pain has been felt and my deepest questions have gone unanswered. But with my hurt still with me, I will choose to live. I hope to find meaningful reasons to live even more fully than before, though I honestly cannot yet see or even imagine what that will look like. With God's help, I'll take a step today and another tomorrow in hopes that such a meaningful life really exists past the bend in the road, far up ahead."

Comparison Trap #3: What I Have vs. What Others Have

Our contentment is undermined by comparing ourselves to other people. You can always find people who are more attractive, wealthier, more successful, and who seem to enjoy more freedoms, better relationships, better physiques, and fewer problems. Their SUV is newer, their complexion is better, and their children are better behaved. They have dream jobs, nicer homes with higher ceilings, fewer health problems, and take incredible vacations.

Forgive me for talking about cars again, but you must know (and this is the truth) that the first word I uttered as a baby was not *mama* or *dada*. It was *car*. One of my prized possessions is a photograph of me as a six-year-old, sitting in the driver's seat of Richard Petty's number 43 legendary race car. I was thrilled that "The King" let me sit in his car, but I was a little disappointed that he wouldn't let me take it for a spin. So what if I couldn't reach the pedals? I have serious auto lust. My wife is not afraid I'll ever leave her for another woman; she's concerned that I might leave her for a Mazda RX-8.

I turned forty while we were living in Greenville, South Carolina. One thing that made turning forty endurable was my earlier declaration that on completing my fourth decade I would buy my first *new* car. I wasn't dreading turning forty—I was looking forward to it. Dorrie insisted that I get all the features that I wanted on the 2000 Honda Accord I was considering. That way, I couldn't have buyer's remorse. So I got the EX model and ordered leather interior, a sunroof, and a spoiler. It's not easy to make a four-door Accord look racy, but I was trying.

Greenville is the home of the BMW Roadster and SUV assembly plant. New BMWs of every model are everywhere, many of them driven by employees who are able to lease them for the price of a Schwinn as a part of their salary package. I considered dropping out of the ministry and working the assembly line. Not really...but if the BMW operations manager in Greenville reads this and thinks the plant and office workers would benefit from having an on-site, full-time chaplain or counselor, I hope he won't hesitate to contact me immediately.

Anyway, I was thrilled with my car. It had new car smell and an amazing stereo. I wanted to sleep in it. Then Stephan moved in directly across from us. He was a BMW employee sent to Greenville from Germany for a two-year assignment. I think Stephan drove a different BMW every month. It was bad enough that his 320i convertible or SUV laughed at my Accord and gave it an inferiority complex, but most of Stephan's friends were also BMW employees transferred from Germany. On weekends his home and backyard was filled with German accents and German beer. That was not the problem. It was all the shiny new BMWs that spilled from his driveway onto the street like we were having an auto show in the neighborhood.

I shouldn't have done it, but I did the touristy thing and I took the tour at the plant where you can see a BMW Roadster being built from beginning to end. The process of quality manufacturing along the assembly line was like a form of embryonic development. I emotionally bonded with this red sports car and when it was birthed at the end of the line I felt like they were taking my baby away. I slumped into my year-old Honda for the drive home. The car seemed average and frumpy. I felt like I had just been on a date out of town with a gorgeous supermodel and was now returning home to where my girlfriend, Bertha, lived.

ANOTHER WAY

Comedienne Joan Rivers was fond of saying, "People who say that money can't buy happiness just don't know where to shop." I became acquainted with a lot of wealthy people in Palm Beach County who would beg to differ. One of the most delightful people that I met and later had the joy of baptizing was Mary Alice Firestone (yes, the Firestone you're thinking of). Married to one of the original Firestone heirs, Mary Alice lived in the Palm Beach Island lap of luxury, down the street from Donald and Marla Trump. There was no accessory, experience, trip, or pleasure that she could not pay cash for. But Mary Alice would be the first to tell you that it did not buy her a happy marriage or enough stuff to make her loneliness go away. MasterCard couldn't keep her marriage together, so she is no longer a Firestone. Sure, she came out pretty well in the court settlement, but that's not where she anchors her security. Her favorite stories to tell are not about exotic trips she took on private yachts, or even about being the homecoming queen at Palm Beach High School many decades ago, when she dated a classmate and football player named Burt Reynolds. Mary Alice's favorite story to tell is about how God changed her life.

> Paul's declaration of contentment silences our sarcasm because it echoes off prison walls.

The Bible says, "Godliness with contentment is great gain" (1 Timothy 6:6). In the same vein, it also says, "Keep your lives free from the love of money and be content with what you have" (Hebrews 13:5). Let those two verses sink in for a moment. Now contrast that to the message of contemporary culture that assures you are always just one purchase away from happiness. Am I saying that you are a carnal, compromising embarrassment to God if you wish for or actually buy a new skirt, jacket, car, or house? What if you linger over the Land's End or Levenger's catalog? Of course not! But just don't be surprised if the buzz you get from the sale is short-lived.

Have you ever noticed that the best part of shopping is in the hunt? The gravitational tug of the shopping bag on our fingers is slightly anticlimatic, isn't it? Even bringing the item home and using it does not have quite the same effect on our adrenaline as did the anticipation of ownership. The real rush is in the search. Yet we keep thinking that this is the purchase that will be different.

Aspiring writers are usually envious of published authors. They imagine that having a book in print by a respected publisher must be like entering the Promised Land, a dreamy landscape where the privileged ones bask in a constant aura of deep satisfaction. Yes, the euphoria of holding your baby in hardback, of seeing it on the shelf at Barnes & Noble, is wonderful in its newness, but the exhilaration wears off. The fact that I have books and articles in print doesn't somehow give me a Teflon coating that prevents frustrations from ever sticking to me.

Writing and creating is indeed wonderfully gratifying and that's probably why I've been doing it since the third grade. It is such an encouragement to hear that something I've published has been helpful to a reader. (Please let me know if that is the case with this book. It's like being a proud parent when you learn that your child has done a good deed.) I do not write in order to get high from the drug of publication. The buzz just doesn't last long enough to motivate me through all the revisions and rewrites. There must be a higher purpose.

So we've established that contentment does not dwell on comparisons, and we've examined the three comparison traps that set us up for discontentment. Let's now consider the second thing that contentment does not do.

CONTENTMENT DOES NOT DEPEND ON CIRCUMSTANCES

The hidden belief underlying discontentment is that if circumstances were changed you would be happy.

- I refuse to be happy unless we move out of this apartment into a house.
- I cannot be happy without being married.
- I can't possibly be happy stuck in this marriage.
- I cannot be happy because of my job.
- I cannot be happy unless the kids are all healthy, well-behaved, and making good grades.
- I refuse to act happy when I've been treated unfairly.
- Who could be content with this medical condition?

What's in your blank? What's your readily available reason for being miserable? If the "My Life Sucks" class had show-and-tell, what would you bring? "My life sucks because _____

_____."

• •

I'm hard-pressed to think of a vehicle that will take you to the land of contentment other than perspective.

• •

Paul claims to have learned to be content "whatever the circumstances." We find ourselves saying in response, "Yeah, sure, Paul—how about test driving my life for a few laps and see how content you are!" But Paul's declaration of contentment silences our sarcasm because it echoes off prison walls. You may feel trapped in some present situation, imprisoned by some undesirable circumstances. Paul was chained to Roman soldiers twenty-four hours a day. Yet he was not held captive by discontentment. Neither did he feel tortured by his circumstances. Perhaps you cannot identify with that kind of victory. At the very least, allow this lesson to spur you on to a search—a search to know Paul's secret.

CONTENTMENT IS THE FRUIT OF PERSPECTIVE

I'm hard-pressed to think of a vehicle that will take you to the land of contentment other than perspective. Without perspective, contentment is a fast-moving target. I'm amazed that fighter jets can land on the small patch of runway painted on aircraft carriers. Imagine if those ships were moving like speed boats and zigzagging like butterflies. Without the steadying mechanism of perspective, contentment is just that difficult to land on.

Paul's extraordinary attitude came from a remarkable perspective. Perspective is the lens through which you view your world. Perspective is the way you interpret and respond to your life. Below are four unique perspectives that Paul used to view his circumstances:

- God's glory is more important than my comfort or success (Philippians 1:20; 2:16–17).
- My true citizenship is not here (Philippians 3:20).
- This world cannot contain my highest ambition (Philippians 3:7–8).
- What other people think of me is not of the highest importance (Philippians 1:15–18).

You can look up these verses in the book of Philippians and feel their impact, knowing Paul was speaking his true feelings and attitude. He wasn't covering up or trying to impress his audience. Before we leave this subject, let's consider one more vital truth about contentment.

CONTENTMENT IS LEARNED BEHAVIOR

Paul said, "I've *learned* to be content whatever the circumstances," and "I've *learned* the secret of being content" (Philippians 4:11–12). Don't think that some people just have the personality and the natural capacity to be content and others don't. If you know anything about Paul, you know he was not a laid-back kind of guy. He was very intense. He was goal oriented and very passionate. Contentment was not a feature of his original persona, which just happened to get Christianized along with the rest of him. Neither did Paul simply choose by an act of the will to be content. He *learned* to be content.

Think for a moment how learning takes place. Learning is foundational and progressive. For example, in first-grade math you learned addition before you were taught multiplication. You were taught basic subtraction before tackling fractions. You learned your ABCs and then discovered how they worked to make words. You then learned how to form words into logical, grammatically correct sentences. Learning is a step-by-step process; new learning builds on the step of previous understanding. The same is true in the spiritual realm—new learning builds on the step of prior understanding.

When Paul says that he learned to be content, do you think he learned that the day after his conversion? Of course not! It was a process of Paul growing in his knowledge of Christ and the gospel of grace and in his understanding about spiritual warfare, suffering, and the Spirit-controlled life. Through this process he gained considerable insight into the matters of heaven and eternal rewards. Paul's learned contentment was the ripe fruit of perspective.

If Paul can learn contentment, so can we. Here are some things Paul learned that contributed to his contentment:

1. *Paul learned to trust God's goodness.* Paul did not measure God's goodness according to favorable circumstances.
2. *Paul learned to extract meaning even in the midst of difficulty.* The imprisonment provided Paul the opportunity to share the gospel with the Roman guard who likely told others about their conversations.
3. *Paul learned to find causes for celebration.* Paul celebrated his relationship with the Philippians and rejoiced that his imprisonment served to ignite their boldness.

As we close this chapter, I want to share this selection from Emily Perl Kingsley, a mother of a child with a birth defect.

WELCOME TO HOLLAND

I am often asked to describe the experience of raising a child with a disability—to try to help people who have not shared that unique experience to understand it, to imagine how it would feel. It's like this...

When you're going to have a baby, it's like planning a fabulous vacation trip—to Italy. You buy a bunch of guide books and make your wonderful plans. The Coliseum. The Michelangelo David. The gondolas in Venice. You may learn some handy phrases in Italian. It's all very exciting.

After months of eager anticipation, the day finally arrives. You pack your bags and off you go. Several hours later, the plane lands. The stewardess comes in and says, "Welcome to Holland."

"Holland?!?" you say. "What do you mean Holland?? I signed up for Italy! I'm supposed to be in Italy. All my life I've dreamed of going to Italy."

But there's been a change in the flight plan. They've landed in Holland and there you must stay.

The important thing is that they haven't taken you to a horrible, disgusting, filthy place, full of pestilence, famine and disease. It's just a different place.

So you must go out and buy new guide books. And you must learn a whole new language. And you will meet a whole new group of people you would never have met.

It's just a different place. It's slower-paced than Italy, less flashy than Italy. But after you've been there for a while and you catch your breath, you look around...and you begin to notice that Holland has windmills...and Holland has tulips. Holland even has Rembrandts.

But everyone you know is busy coming and going from Italy... and they're all bragging about what a wonderful time they had there. And for the rest of your life, you will say "Yes, that's where I was supposed to go. That's what I had planned."

And the pain of that will never, ever, ever, ever go away...because the loss of that dream is a very very significant loss.

But...if you spend your life mourning the fact that you didn't get to Italy, you may never be free to enjoy the very special, the very lovely things...about Holland.[15]

Do you recognize the similar life change lessons from the apostle Paul?

1. *You don't have to pretend that you're not disappointed with an unmet goal or unfulfilled dream.* If you wind up in Holland instead of Italy, or make it to Italy as Paul did but as a prisoner instead of an evangelist, then you'll be disappointed. Remember we said that contentment allows for disappointment, but it does not give in to immobilizing despair. John Eldredge says, "Being content is not pretending that everything is the way you wish it would be; it is not acting as though you have no wishes. Rather, it is no longer being *ruled* by your desires."[16]

2. *You must learn a new language.* You must learn to be present in your "now." Grieve if you must, but determine to learn a new language of contentment in this unexpected territory. To get stuck in the comparison trap is a sign that you're not learning a new language. Insisting that you cannot be happy because of *X* is your accent from the old dialect. Remember that Paul *learned* to be content—it did not come naturally and it did not come quickly. Are you willing to begin?

3. *You must find special people, places, and moments to celebrate.* Holland has windmills, tulips, and Rembrandts. Paul extracted positive outcomes from his undesirable situation and recognized new possibilities (Philippians 1:12–14). You can become fixated by what's wrong or what's missing from your Holland vacation and stay in your room, or you can become a tourist, an explorer of this new place and season you're in. There are existing relationships to appreciate and new ones to pursue. There are unique places, things, events, moments, and opportunities awaiting those who would venture out of their solemn room.

We all have our disabled children, our dream of Italy, our disappointment with Holland. The question is now that we find ourselves in Holland instead of Italy, how will we respond?

9

From Anxiety to Peace: the Alchemy of Prayer

Worrying was my mother's way. She fretted about the weather, the cost of groceries, the washing machine breaking down, the Tecumseh River being dirtied by the paper mill in Adams valley, the price of new clothes, and everything under the sun. To my mother, the world was a vast quilt whose stitches were always coming undone. Her worrying somehow worked like a needle, tightening those dangerous seams. If she could imagine events through to their worst tragedy, then she seemed to have some kind of control over them. As I said, it was her way. My father could throw up a fistful of dice to make a decision, but my mother had an agony for every hour.

–Robert McCammon[17]

One of the best-selling books from the '90s was *Don't Sweat the Small Stuff.* Its author tapped into the national panic regarding the seemingly consuming stress of everyday life. With all our technological advances, we are a culture that has discovered that the evil twin of rapid development may be rampant anxiety. Therapists are not only treating hundreds of thousands of adults with anxiety disorders, but are also pressed into treating anxiety in young children, most of whom are from financially secure homes but are demonstrating symptoms not even seen in children from war-torn nations! As adults we face issues regarding career, finances, marriage, children, aging parents, health, and schedule overload, just to name a few.

In anxious moments, it often feels like the appropriate time and place to erect a monument with a waving flag to the undeniable and eternal truth that my life sucks. All around me is chaos, all I feel is doom. Into that chaos the apostle Paul writes, "Do not be anxious about anything..." (Philippians 4:6) We hear this and something inside us wants to retort, "Oh yeah? Get real, buddy." The subtitle of *Don't Sweat the Small Stuff* reassures that "it's all small stuff." But when your eighty-year-old mother who lives three hundred miles away has fallen and broken her hip, it's not small stuff. When your husband is laid off, it's not small stuff. When your daughter is separating from her husband, it's not small stuff. And when all that is happening simultaneously, it's not small stuff!

Paul's therapeutic counsel for anxiety would hardly be credible if not for the fact that he is modeling the treatment plan and demonstrating its success. Remember that Paul is in prison and facing possible execution. When a man is inching his way along death row and says, "You don't have to be a prisoner of worry," it makes you want to at least hear him out.

The word *anxiety* will be used frequently in this chapter. Dr. Archibald Hart distinguishes between worry-anxiety and stress-anxiety. The anxiety most people suffer from is a function of "high adrenaline, caused by over-extension and stress, which depletes the brain's natural tranquilizers and sets the stage for high anxiety."[18] Worry-anxiety, on the other hand, according to Dr. William Backus is an "overestimation of the probability of danger and exaggeration of its degree of terribleness."[19] It is the worry brand of anxiety that Paul addresses and that will be our focus.

Life is often a three-ring circus of major concerns. From the following arenas, rank your top three according to what currently provokes the most worry in your life.

____ Finances	____ Boyfriend/Girlfriend
____ Career	____ Ex-spouse
____ Marriage	____ Family member
____ Parent(s)	____ Friendship
____ Children	____ Major Decision
____ Health	____ Other:
	_____

For each area you selected answer the following questions: 1) What is the core problem or concern you have about this area? 2) What do you imagine or fear will happen regarding this problem? Keep your answers in mind as you read the rest of this chapter.

> The anticipation of future trouble or the fear of present trouble provokes us to worry.

Someone once quipped, "Life is like living in a room full of dynamite with a monkey running around with a blowtorch. It's not a matter of *if*, but just *when*." That's a rather fatalistic view of the future. But while it overstates the case, the imagery does illustrate Jesus' declaration that "in this world you will have trouble" (John 16:33). Even when life's seas are calm, experience tells us that the storms are coming eventually. The anticipation of future trouble or the fear of present trouble provokes us to worry. Indeed, the dictionary defines worry as the "mental distress or agitation resulting from concern, usually from something pending or anticipated."[20]

To the Philippians Paul wrote:

> Rejoice in the Lord always. I will say it again: Rejoice! Let your gentleness be evident to all. The Lord is near. Do not be anxious about anything, but in everything, by prayer and petition, with thanksgiving, present your requests to God. And the peace of God, which transcends all understanding, will guard your hearts and your minds in Christ Jesus. (Philippians 4:4–7)

Too often this passage has been used as a condemnation of worry, which has often served to make some people feel spiritually weak on top of their anxiety. But as we'll see, the passage is not so much a condemnation of worry (or the worrier) as it is a prescription for dealing with worry.

> The passage is not so much a condemnation of worry (or the worrier) as it is a prescription for dealing with worry.

With Philippians 4:6–7 being our foundation passage, we are about to examine some related verses that will shine light on the subject through the means of a word study. I realize that you may not share my fascination with the etymology of words, but hang in there. I'll make it worth your effort. Note that one of the things we'll do is search for and draw application from verses containing these two Greek words: *merimnao* (anxiety) and *phroneo* (concern).[21]

We'll start with the verse above, Philippians 4:6: "Do not be **anxious** (*merimnao*) about anything." Now consider this statement in Philippians. 4:10: "I rejoice greatly in the Lord that at last you have renewed your **concern** (*phroneo*) for me." From these two sentences it seems to work out nicely—it's okay and good to be concerned, but it's bad to be anxious.

But let's turn back to Philippians 2:19–20: "I hope in the Lord to send Timothy to you soon, that I also may be cheered when I receive news about you. I have no one else like him, who *takes a genuine interest* in your welfare" (emphasis added). The phrase that is translated into the English "takes a genuine interest" is actually the Greek word for **anxiety** (*merimnao*). Therefore, the verse could more accurately be translated, "I have no one else like him who worries about you." Hmmm, perhaps this is a commendable worry?

Now look at a line from another of Paul's letters, 2 Corinthians 11:28: "Besides everything else, I face daily the pressure of my **concern** for all the churches." Your Bible may translate it "concern" but in the

Greek New Testament you will not find the word for **concern** (*phroneo*) but the word for **anxiety** (*merimnao*). Well, maybe it's okay to worry about the welfare of others, but self-centered worry is bad. But wait, Paul said not to be anxious about anything. We have a dilemma here. Is Paul contradicting himself? Is the Scripture contradicting itself? It is not a contradiction when you understand that Paul is not making a wholesale

•••••••••••••••••••••

The present is the only place you live and the only time period you can operate in.

•••••••••••••••••••••

condemnation of worry but is offering a solution for dealing with this common problem.

The verb tense for *merimnao* in Philippians 4:6 suggests ongoing worry without interruption. Actually, the verse could be translated: "Don't *just* worry…" In other words, don't ob-

sess and become fixated in worry. Don't just give in to worry and ride it like a treadmill to nowhere! Paul understands human nature, and his own experiences tell him that life in a fallen world produces anxious moments. However, being absolutely immobilized by worry is counter-productive. Jesus saw the futility of worry when he said, "Who of you by worrying can add a single hour to his life?" (Matthew 6:27). I am fond of telling my clients that guilt and shame (which are fixated on the past) and worry (which is largely fixated on the future) are all quite use-less unless they motivate them to do something different in the present! The present is the only place you live and the only time period you can operate in.

If spiritual x-rays could be taken they would reveal that chronic worry is causing much of our pain. But Paul has much more to recommend here than just a slogan that says, "don't do it." Paul offers a viable alternative to full-blown and useless panic. He insists that prayer is one of the best methods of defusing the anxiety bomb because it disconnects one of the wires that powers it. Paul is essentially saying, "Don't merely worry, but let anxiety be the warning light on your dashboard that tells you to pull over, get out, and go to your knees instead of the liquor cabinet. Don't just worry—let your anxiety be a burglar alarm that warns you something's trying to steal your peace and joy." Paul's counsel is to fight the thief on our knees. The advice is not a trite, "Well, just pray about it, brother." Rather, it is an exhortation to meaningful communion with God.

Why does this work? How is prayer effective in replacing worry with peace? First, one of the smartest things you can do when you're anxious is to find someone who is really calm and is a good listener, as opposed to someone who mirrors your anxiety ("Oh my gosh, you're doomed! What are you going to do?") or someone who hijacks your anxiety ("That's nothing. Let me tell you about the time I was fired right before Christmas"). I hope that you have a friend who is genuinely a good and calm listener. When in prayer, you are in the presence of Jehovah-Shalom, the Lord our Peace.

God is at peace in himself, and in his presence there is peace. The most repeated negative command in Scripture is "fear not." It appears 365 times—one for each day of the year—and is usually followed by "for I am with you." God would have us understand that factoring in his presence always changes the equation.

Second, in prayer you regain perspective and truth. Remember that genuine prayer is a dialogue. Prayer that attacks worry doesn't work because of catharsis—just pour your heart out and then you'll feel better. Prayer is not just a spiritual dumping ground or a laxative for emotional constipation. In Western churches we are fond of saying that prayer is simply talking to God. The intent is good—to counter any paralyzing belief that prayer is complicated and should only be attempted by experts. But that's only half the conversation. Prayer isn't just doing all the talking; it's also about listening.

Look at the before and after picture in Mark 14:32–41. Jesus went into the garden of Gethsemane deeply distressed and troubled. He came out bold and ready to face his betrayer and the cross. How do you explain the change? What I really would like to know about Jesus' prayer in the garden is what he heard. What did his Father say that so reassured

Jesus that he arose resolutely from prayer? I don't know what the Father said, but I would suggest that it was more important than what the Son said, in terms of bringing a renewal of peace.

Through this dialogue of prayer, truth brings perspective to our myopic view of our problem. All we can see is gloom, and all we can hear is doom. Meanwhile, God is in our peripheral vision waving for our attention so he can whisper reassuring truth. My clients often hear this phrase from me: "Yes, your concern is valid and your pain is true. But it's not the only truth." Dear Sir, it is true that your being laid off could hardly come at a worse time, but that is not the only truth. Yes Ma'am, the betrayal is a painful truth, and it would make life hopeless if it were the only truth... but it's not.

> My clients often hear this phrase from me: "Yes, your concern is valid and your pain is true. But it's not the only truth."

The inside of a Honda Accord isn't exactly the Mount of Transfiguration, but I had a conversation with God while gliding along U.S. 31 on the way to a Chamber of Commerce breakfast meeting. I felt inclined to knock on God's door on behalf of a friend who told me he was burdened by pressing demands. My conversation with God went something like this...

"If Byron says he's feeling pressure, then he's really feeling pressure! God, I don't know what to ask you to do. I don't know what kind of pressure he's facing and feeling."

"Ramon, when you feel pressure, besides stress, what do you feel when the heat's on?"

"Hmmm.... I feel afraid."

"Afraid of what? Think about it."

"Different things. I'm afraid of failing, afraid of not having enough..."

"Enough of what?"

"Enough time, enough money, enough support, enough help, enough interest, enough attendance, enough cooperation, enough energy, enough ability. Afraid of not having enough of something to get the job done right or done at all, not enough to make ends meet. Sometimes I feel like the plate spinning guy in the circus. I don't know that I can keep all my fifty-seven personal and professional plates spinning? Sometimes I'm afraid that..."

"What was that crashing sound?"

"Make that 56 plates."

"So, you're afraid of not having what you need, or at least afraid of not having what you think you need?"

"Yeah, I'm afraid of not having enough of what I need so I can produce."

"Interesting. Produce what?"

"Results. And no, it's not about producing results so I look good, if that's what you're thinking. I'm not an approval or applause addict. Results are about everything coming out right. God, I'm afraid of coming up short, not measuring up, okay? I said it already, I'm afraid of failing. I'm afraid of being mediocre. I'm afraid of not being able to keep up. I'm a good counselor and a good writer, but what if that's not enough to take care of my family? I have to be a good businessman now too. When it comes right down to it, for me, what it all boils down to is that I'm afraid of failing as a provider for my family. I'm afraid that my wife has put her trust in me and I'm going to let her down. God, I'm afraid of making her afraid. Does any of that make sense?"

"It does. Anything else that you fear?"

"The unknown."

"The unknown?"

"Yeah, I fear the unknown, the uncertainty. I'm afraid of what could happen or afraid of what won't happen that needs to happen."

"Ramon, remember what David said about where he went and where I showed up, that there is no place in time, location, or experience that I'm not already there with the coffee made when you arrive. Ramon, if you knew, really knew, that I was going to be fully present and engaged in the mysterious unknown and uncertainty of your future, what else would you need to know?"

"Huh?"

"If you knew that I promised to be with you wherever, whenever, for whatever...and if you knew I would keep my promise, of what thing would you need to be afraid?"

"Nothing?"

"Yeah, nothing."

"I think I get it. But you know you'll need to remind me of this conversation from time to time. Short memory."

"Glad to. Anything else on your mind?"

"Well, God, I was going to pray for Byron."

"You just did."

"I was talking about me, my pressures, my fears. I didn't get around to asking you to do anything for Byron."

"Do you think the source and core of your pressures and your fears are that much different than his?"

"Maybe not, but I still didn't ask you to do anything for him."

"I'm running a two-for-one special today."

"Thanks. Anything else you want to tell me before I go inside to this meeting?"

"Yeah, tell Byron about our conversation this morning. Let him know I'm thinking about him and I'll see to it that he has what he needs when he needs it."

"Okay. I'll do that." (I did.)

Before closing this chapter, let's return to Paul's prescription for worry. The doctor's orders are that the one who is anxious should pray. Certainly one is encouraged to enlist others to pray for him, but the verse implies that "the peace of God, which transcends all understanding" (Philippians 4:7) is a result, a by-product, of prayer by the one in need.

But prayer cannot be systematized, delegated, or outsourced. I can hire a personal trainer to coach me, but he cannot lift the weights for me. In the matter of prayer nothing short of *my* engagement alters *my* condition. Often you may hear someone pray for a friend, "Lord, give Jim the peace that surpasses all understanding." While God is certainly able to answer that intercession (based at least on Philippians 4:6–7), the burden is placed squarely on the anxious person to pray. I'm not minimizing the power of intercession and the effect of praying for others. I'm just directing your attention to Paul's implied principle of praying for peace—it's a do-it-yourself project.

Another way to think of it, this remarkable peace, is not as a prayer request, but as a prayer result. Couples in love don't focus their conversations on the topic of emotional intimacy. ("Hey honey, let's converse about the dynamics of reciprocal disclosure.") Instead, they naturally share with each other on a deep, personal level, and the intimacy is present and grows.

Recently I placed an order online to have a book sent to my dad for his birthday. The sole interaction took place between me and Amazon, and then Amazon delivered the gift right to my dad's door. God isn't offering to operate like Amazon and deliver peace parcels to unsuspecting friends and family members. The wording of the passage implies that the transaction is to be a direct exchange between the worried soul and the Prince of Peace. The result of such a focused prayer encounter is a peace that will "guard your hearts and your minds" (Philippians 4:7). Drawing from a military analogy, the verb to guard (*phroureo*) recalls a military garrison stationed inside the city employed to protect its citizens. Thus the peace of God residing within the heart and mind of the praying believer acts as a guard against the intruding warriors of anxious thought.

10

Baggage Claim:
Getting Past the Past

The question, when will my life not suck? is more of a statement than a question. It's a frustrated protest of current conditions, not so much a genuine hope for better days.

The past can be an antique mall of old hurts, wounds, offenses, rejections, neglect, abuse, lack of opportunity, missed opportunities, and squelched dreams. In the vintage baggage section you can find mocked aspirations, conspiracies, sabotage, prejudice, poor health, insufficient funds, unsupportive parents, bad dates, evil ex-spouses, and rebellious children. That's just a sampling from the bottomless pit of bad things that have happened to us. Then there's an entirely different aisle for our own past crimes—sins, failures, bad decisions, and stupid mistakes— that we profess still bring us suffering or punishment. Hold onto your shopping basket; an enthusiastic shopper can find plenty of items to justify the self-pitying claim: "See, look at this! My whole life has sucked."

Let me hasten to say that I don't mean to make light of painful experiences in your past. As a pastor and therapist I've been given a front-row seat to unimaginable suffering. I have often left a home, a hospital, a jail, or my counseling office, shook my head, and thought, "I don't know if I could survive if I had to endure *that*." I fully recognize that the past has profound influence on our present experience. But a large measure of the past's power and control in our lives is authorized by us. Some of us are so weighed down by our past that we are practically carrying our tombstone to announce that we are no longer really living—they just haven't buried our body yet. The dates of our birth and death are already etched into the granite. The final date was when we were fired, when the affair was discovered, when our spouse left, when the business failed, when the accident happened, when our loved one died, when our child rebelled, when we declared bankruptcy, when the house went into foreclosure, when he started drinking, or when we got that phone call. We're the walking dead, emotionally and spiritually hollowed-out, just waiting for our body and the coroner to make it official.

> I fully recognize that the past has profound influence on our present experience. But a large measure of the past's power and control in our lives is authorized by us.

"But one thing I do: forgetting what lies behind and reaching forward to what lies ahead, I press on toward the goal" (Philippians 3:13–14 NASB). I've always had a fondness for that verse because it has my last name in it. But more importantly it reveals Paul's approach to engaging his past, present, and future.

PAUL'S ORIENTATION TO HIS PAST

If you read the section preceding the verse just mentioned, you'll see Paul writing about the status that he achieved and enjoyed as a religious leader in the community. Paul was well-bred, well-educated, and well-groomed for affluence and influence. Then Paul made a stunning denouncement of his prior status. You can read it for yourself in Philippians 3:4–8, but permit me a Presson paraphrase: "I consider my previous life waste material, pure garbage, and cow patties compared to my life now." The potential hindrance of Paul's past would not have been how bad it was, but how good it was. He had financial security at home and status in the community. Now he is in jail and he says that this persecuted life is far better than the celebrity circles he walked in before. Either Paul is a masochist or in a state of detached denial, or he has developed a remarkable coping mechanism in light of his lost life of ease. Paul's attitude stands in stark contrast to that of the Israelites who constantly complained to Moses about how much better off they were as slaves in Egypt compared to being freed tourists in the desert. Paul does not allow the trappings of his former life to hang on him and weigh him down in the present.

> Either Paul is a masochist or in a state of detached denial, or he has developed a remarkable coping mechanism in light of his lost life of ease.

For you, perhaps like Paul, the past was a comfortable and secure place, and there's nothing wrong with that. But things may be different now. The landscape has changed and nothing looks and feels the same. Something was lost, something really good. And now you're stuck here in the present. You were living in a nice house, but that was before the divorce settlement. You weren't in love with your job last year, but at least you had one. You never had supermodel breasts, but at least they were yours and not cancer's. Your daughter was an angel and then she went off to college to become an alcoholic dropout. Actually, the past wasn't really as fantastic as you remember it. Would you care to hear a recording of all your complaints during those years? I'm guessing you weren't oozing enthusiasm and gratitude. But the past seems like paradise compared to the current terrain of hell. (I recommend that you review the comparison traps in chapter 8 again.)

> Whether we feel like we were gunned down by some kind of sniper, or we despise having shot ourselves in the leg, the desire for healing and for freedom is the same.

There is a legitimate grief when good things are damaged or completely lost. God is not on the sideline snickering at your grimacing pain saying, "C'mon, rub some dirt on it; don't be a wimp. Run the next play!" But ultimately the dominant question of your life must transition from *why* or *what happened* to *now what*. Otherwise, you start wearing the tombstone pendant.

Perhaps for you the pain of the past is not the grieving of Camelot, but the screaming of Hades. The past is a horror film on continuous play. The abuse has stopped, but the images seem implanted into your brain. There has been victory over the addiction, but that hasn't stopped the demons from urging you to come out and play. The question is not so much how to let go of a romanticized past, but how to amputate a terribly diseased one. Whether we feel like we were gunned down by some kind of sniper, or we despise having shot ourselves in the leg, the desire for healing and for freedom is the same. Am I destined to be defined by my past and paralyzed by it?

Paul was able to pull away from the grip of memory and past influences because he was able to focus on the possibilities the future held. When I'm feeling stuck emotionally, my willpower's pep talking, butt kicking, and "shoulding" all over myself have seldom dislodged me. It is envisioning a preferred future, striving for a desire or goal, and reaching for something of value that lures me from inertia and pulls me toward tomorrow. Maybe there is a reason we have tow trucks and not push trucks. We are more easily and successfully pulled toward something good than pushed out of something bad.

Releasing the past does not imply striving for amnesia. On the contrary, there is valuable material from the past that we need to bring with us on the journey into the present and into the future. We learn much from our personal history, and there is treasure to mine from it. Our prior experiences are part of our navigational equipment. It was Paul's position as a Pharisee and his extraordinary grasp of Old Testament law that uniquely positioned him not only as a stunning convert but an effective apostle. It was Paul's education and astute mind that poised him to be a brilliant theologian, writer, preacher, missionary, church planter, and pastor. His influence on Christendom is second only to that of Christ himself. It was Paul's fiery personality that was channeled into the strengths of a revolutionary who stirred either a revival or a riot almost everywhere he went. While Paul considered his past gains as losses in light of his new relationship with Christ, God didn't waste one ounce of what Paul considered of little value to cling to. This is no contradiction. Paul was not declaring his past useless, but announcing that it was now woefully inadequate in defining him.

Does your history include anything that you think would negatively define you, or anything you currently allow to define you? I often meet adults who feel shame because of an unwanted divorce. It's almost as if they imagine they are wearing the scarlet letter, a big red *D* monogrammed on their clothing for the entire world to see. And oftentimes they most feel the silent but stinging judgment in the church. Even if the separated or divorced spouse was abandoned, abused, or rejected for an adulterous affair, that spouse still often feels like the church has pronounced his or her marriage a failure.

It is my experience that women, especially, may internalize a failure label for a tragic marriage outcome or a rebellious child. Wives and mothers feel the homespun relationships reflect on them positively or negatively. I've observed that it is often difficult for middle-aged women to differentiate their worth from the choices and behaviors of their adult children. The first place their mind goes is "what did I do wrong?" and "I must not have been a very good mother." There is no self-inflicted wound more painful than a woman pronouncing herself a bad mother.

> Beware of labeling yourself, and resist labeling from others.

There are no words that will cut her deeper than to hear her maternal performance condemned by others, and no one's judgment is as deadly as her child's.

Beware of labeling yourself, and resist labeling from others. Calvin Miller makes a strong point about the foolishness of labels: "No man may burn a label into flesh and make it stay when heaven disagrees."[22] On more than one occasion I've had clients refer to themselves as damaged goods—a self-description that I pounce on like a cheetah. Think about that phrase for a moment. It implies something that people bring back for a refund or exchange, something thrown away, or if lucky, marked down for quick sale. A person feeling this way cannot hope for genuine love in a healthy relationship, not when the only prospects will be junk dealers and garage sale shoppers.

If you insist upon using the damaged goods concept, then at least accept the reality that you are in good company. All of us are damaged goods on some level.

Does anybody make it to adulthood without flaws? Paul wrote that "we have this treasure in jars of clay to show that this all-surpassing power is from God and not from us" (2 Corinthians 4:7). The clay jar metaphor implies a reference to more than just our bodies as fleshly external containers. Paul is saying that ordinary people are what God chooses to bring for show-and-tell. We, the plain, the unimpressive, the broken, the flawed, are his chosen billboards to advertise his extraordinary glory and power.

By now you have likely heard and probably have seen on YouTube the amazing story of Paul Potts, an employee of The Carphone Warehouse in South Wales who took the stage in the 2007 edition of *Britain's Got Talent*, a show similar to *American Idol*. His frumpy body was tucked into a boring navy suit; he lacked good looks and apparently access to good dental care. His nervous smile and rigid posture betrayed any attempt at confidence. When asked about his selection, he simply said, "I'm here to sing opera." The judges' skepticism and dread couldn't have been more obvious. The music began, Paul opened his mouth of crooked teeth…and the sound that came out was astonishing. The notes, range, clarity, and resonance were breathtaking. In a matter of seconds applause and tears flowed in the audience as a Pavarotti-like voice came gently forth and then shook the auditorium. A standing ovation made his final notes barely audible to viewers. The judges were stunned and clearly moved, among them Simon Cowell. The absence of professional pedigree and his unimpressive exterior made the performance all the more incredible. Simon spoke for all viewers when he in understated fashion said, "I wasn't expecting that."

SCUBA LESSON

A scuba diver seeks to achieve a weightlessness that allows his body to move almost effortlessly through the depths and over the reefs. There are several factors that wage war against that weightless glide. Water makes the body buoyant and thus resistant to hovering in one spot sixty feet beneath the surface. The scuba gear, especially the tank, is heavy, and while the added weight aids in the descent, it typically either fails to eliminate buoyancy or it causes the diver to sink like a concrete block (depending on the size and weight of the diver). To complicate the equation, there is the water pressure difference near the surface as compared with ninety feet from the ocean floor.

The diver wears two pieces of equipment that collaborate to achieve the ideal buoyancy. A variable weight belt helps with the descent and with remaining at the desired depth. Meanwhile, the buoyancy vest can be inflated or deflated with the ideal amount of air. You don't want to be so heavy that you drop to the bottom like an anchor and can barely move. Neither do you want to be so light that you are constantly drifting upwards, fighting to stay down. In addition to ruining the pleasure of the dive, this overexertion causes you to use up your air supply more quickly. (I learned this the hard way when I ran out of air at sixty feet during a dive off Palm Beach.)

> You and I must think accurately about the past and the future in order to avoid being either immobilized or ineffective in the present.

While the weight belt cannot really be altered during the dive, the diver can make frequent adjustments and fine tunings of his buoyancy vest to achieve desired weightlessness. Even apart from the beauty and wonder of the deep sea world, being weightless is an amazing experience—like being in outer space with zero gravity. As you stand up and move to the edge of the rocking boat, the heavy and bulky scuba gear makes you feel like a spastic and obese turtle with giant webbed duck feet. Then moments after cannonballing into the water, you become as graceful as the brilliant fish around you.

I meet people all the time who seem terribly weighed down with their past, as though they had jumped into the present with a heavy weight belt but no buoyancy vest. Or more accurately, they are wearing the vest and don't know how to use it. The past is nothing but concrete blocks in their pockets, and they seem either unable or unwilling to inflate the vest to provide some relief. The buoyancy vest represents the future, the possibilities and opportunities that exist and the vision to move toward them. Some people live as though heaviness is the only option, that buoyancy isn't really possible, so the vest and the future are mostly irrelevant.

A diver is negotiating the variables of weight and buoyancy to achieve a position where he can be fully present in the moment and enjoy the dive. Likewise, Paul has a correct perspective regarding the past and the future, and that assists his effectiveness in the present. You and I must think accurately about the past and the future in order to avoid being either immobilized or ineffective in the present. Just as it is possible to overinflate the vest, it is possible to be so focused on future goals and dreams that we become irresponsible in our present duties.

Paul declares that with his past behind him and a promising future ahead of him, his present job is to press on. To live well in the present, you need proper perspective—a view that holds your past lightly in one hand and your future firmly in the other. Paul keeps moving forward and perseveres. Sometimes the moving forward is slow, but it's forward. Sometimes it's two steps forward and a step backward, but it's still forward.

Many years ago singer-songwriter Billy Sprague's fiancée was killed in an auto accident, and Billy grieved for years. To his credit, he continued to write music and play concerts, but his heart remained broken inside him. Later he wrote a song about his journey toward hope and healing entitled "Press On." To illustrate how feeble progress is at times he included the lyric, "Sometimes I found that faith meant just tying my shoes." Billy will tell you that there were days when just getting out of bed and getting dressed was a victory.

One Sunday at my North Carolina church, one of my single adults informed me that he was going to run his first marathon. The next Sunday I looked for him to ask how he fared in the race. He was late to class and was walking gingerly. It wasn't until after class that I was able to catch Bruce (which wasn't hard in his condition) and ask him, "So, how did it go? How'd you do?" I'll never forget his response: "I finished ahead of everyone who quit."

The past few years I've participated in the Country Music Half Marathons in Nashville. Each year my percentage of the thirteen miles I spent walking rather than running has increased. But then I've never set goals on my race times. My objective is simply to finish. And I do...ahead of everyone who quits. Each year I'm impressed by the number of extremely overweight adults who shout down all the reasons why they can't do a half marathon and silence the critical voice inside that exclaims how foolish they will look compared to all the fit people.

> Success never comes simply because of something; it comes despite something.

They show up and go for it. Huffing, puffing, chafing, jiggling, and sweating profusely, they keep going. Just completing the thirteen-mile trek is as much a victory for them as it is for the first-place finisher, maybe more of a victory. After all, the elite professional runners are expected to finish well; no one expects a rotund middle-aged woman to even lace up the Nikes. Success never comes simply because of something; it comes despite something. Perseverance will always be in spite of something. If you push forward there will always be something pushing back. There will always be resistance of some kind from some source.

RESISTANCE AND GROWTH

There is no growth apart from overcoming resistance. That is true personally, vocationally, emotionally, spiritually, and physically. The principle of overcoming resistance is why weight training builds muscles and strength. The weights are just there to add resistance, which the muscles strain to overcome. The strain against resistance changes the muscle fibers, actually breaking them down initially. As the muscle fibers are repaired they are changed and strengthened beyond their original state.

Whether you are seeking to reduce your blood pressure or increase your income, write a book or right a wrong, lose weight or find some balance, overcome a fear or underspend your budget, you will encounter resistance. Resistance will show up in the form of negative thoughts, self-defeating beliefs, poor health, low energy, competing demands, attractive options, insufficient funds, lack of time, lack of social support, and perhaps even criticism. Excuses for giving up and reasons for not even starting will be available in abundance.

Paul is up off the couch, and he's going for it. He's a man on a mission who has encountered constant resistance from every angle. He's had health issues, been beaten severely and injured, been arrested and imprisoned. He has regularly faced opposition by the Jewish hierarchy, the Roman government, unbelievers everywhere, and Christian believers in many places. He's lacked shelter, money, and provisions. Furthermore, Paul understands that he faces an unseen and sinister Enemy that resists him at every turn and is hell-bent on his defeat.

Something I've observed in my clients (and in myself) is a tendency to start things by forming a negative hypothesis: "I've never caught a break," "You can't trust anyone," "Corporate is just out to use everybody," "All men/women/bosses/employees/salesmen, etc., are alike." Our hypotheses turn out to be amazingly accurate because, once formed, we continually find evidence to support and confirm them. If your hypothesis is "something goes wrong for me every day," how long do you think you'll have to be awake on any given day before your prediction comes true? Just finding the box of Pop Tarts empty on a Monday morning confirms it. "Oh yeah, this week's off to a great start!"

You're probably wondering what this has to do with resolving your past. Just this: we don't form our hypotheses out of thin air, but from experience. We deduce that past experiences are reliable indicators of what we can expect in the future. We conclude that those past experiences are trying to teach us how the world works, how life is, and what people are like. But do good teachers make us cynical, bitter, and suspicious? Is it wisdom that makes us so cautious that we suppress dreams and blockade our heart? "Maybe not," you say, "but I won't be fooled again!" Ah, there it is. We've just removed the iron mask of fatalism to find behind it the fearful face of self-protection. So I prefer to remain jaded rather than risk being tricked, disappointed, or hurt again. I'll be an emotional toxic waste dump because the company, the government, the military, the ex-spouse (take your pick) screwed me over.

As Paul would tell us, dealing with our past is not making it blank like a shaken Etch A Sketch®, erasing all traces of history and its influences. Rather, it is demanding that the past maintain its rank, refusing to allow it to promote itself and take authority over our present and our future.

11

Sour Gripes
Make the Best Whine

*The mind is its own place, and in itself can make a Heaven of
Hell, a Hell of Heaven.*

—John Milton, *Paradise Lost*

Have you noticed how the person with the sucky life insists on letting everyone know how much their sucky life sucks? All the time. You dread or even avoid asking, how are you doing? You know the tune that is going to be played. The first note is a heavy sigh followed by a song in minor chords and depressing lyrics.

> Do everything without complaining or arguing, so that you may
> become blameless and pure, children of God without fault in a
> crooked and depraved generation, in which you shine like stars in
> the universe. (Philippians 2:14–15)

Did you catch that? Paul thinks not complaining and arguing is linked with being blameless and pure? When I think of qualifications for being blameless and pure, I think of not cheating, stealing, lying, driving while drunk, abusing a child, or dealing drugs. Being blameless and pure means being a politician who isn't corrupt, a man who doesn't cheat on his wife, or an employee who doesn't embezzle. It means not being an athlete who fails a drug test two months after being arrested on a weapons charge outside a strip club the same year he is on probation for assaulting his pregnant girlfriend. It means not being addicted to pornography and not punching out the umpire at a Little League game. That's blameless and pure stuff. Not complaining and arguing? Not only does that seem nitpicky, but Paul fails to realize that complaining and arguing is an American pastime. If it were a sanctioned Olympic sport, the U.S. would have no competition for the gold medal. If you're skeptical that this is true, you must be listening to soft rock instead of talk radio.

Indeed, the Constitution allows for a freedom of speech in this country that few if any other nations can match. Think of it: the government relentlessly protects the vocal rights of citizens to viciously bash it. I don't know about you, but I've never felt quite so secure in a relationship that I've readily defended the privilege of verbally abusing me. Our country welcomes debate at every level of election and policy making. It's all we've ever known, so we take it for granted. But there are suppressed and oppressed people in other nations who would be quick to remind us that the American style is the exception.

But there is another factor that likely adds to our thick complaining accent. It is our abundance as the wealthiest nation on earth. You may not think of yourself as wealthy, but if you own a car then by worldwide standards you are quite rich. If you own a home, then compared to the global norm you are filthy rich. You have access to clean drinking water? Welcome to the elite ranks. You have indoor plumbing? You're upper crust. Despite the rising costs, you have access to professional medical care, right? Guess what percentage of the world's population can say that? You cannot imagine living without your cell phone, iPod, Blackberry, laptop, and cable television, right? Please step over here to the privileged few. "But those are norms in America," you say. "I can't help that I was born and raised here!" You're absolutely right, and I'll have something to say about the "frame of reference factor" in a moment.

Because we have it so good, we become dissatisfied with the familiar, and angry about the imperfect. Collectively we are the diner in an exquisite restaurant who indignantly returns the beef bourguignonne because it is not seasoned to our liking. Furthermore, as mentioned in chapter 8, the success of the American economy (and now global economy) depends upon consumer dissatisfaction. Whatever you have, you don't have the newest, the best, the updated, the upgraded, the fastest, the most powerful, most popular, most reliable, the rarest, the sleekest, the easiest to use, the most eco-friendly, ergonomic, the highest rated, the most effective, the biggest, the smallest, the clearest, or the one with the most features.

> Because we have it so good, we become dissatisfied with the familiar, and angry about the imperfect.

Our frame of reference (or perspective) holds a tremendous influence on our expectations and level of contentment. Therefore, it stands to reason that the frame of reference factor comes into play in the arena of complaint. Similar to the comparison traps noted in chapter 8, our frames of reference are the comparison points that help determine what is acceptable or unacceptable for us. Let me illustrate with a recent example. I'm acquainted with a newlywed whose wife is tall, slender, and attractive. However, this upscale gym owner is (by his own admission) obsessed with his own physical fitness, and much of his clientele are female athletes and models. His wife's passion for exercise cannot possibly match his, and she is not a replica of the surgically enhanced, tanned and toned hotties that bend and stretch in his gym. It probably doesn't help that this lifelong athlete's mom has always been nutrition conscious and has kept herself in remarkable shape with self-discipline in her eating and exercise. His older sister is an athlete and head-turner as well. In addition, Brad's work with professional football players has often placed him in the company of their trophy wives.

Do you see Brad's frame of reference for relating to women? His collective vision taken from his family of origin right up to the present atmosphere of his daily work is one of bronzed blondes with flat, smooth abs and firmly curved buttocks. That's reality to him. Despite the fact that most men could only fantasize about having a wife as attractive as Brad's, he is not so secretly annoyed by her "undisciplined nutritional habits" and "inconsistent workouts." While he recognizes and appreciates her many fine personal qualities and her beauty, he has trouble looking at her and not seeing the five or ten pounds that she could lose here or the firming she could do there to "really be her best." Because it is impeding his marital satisfaction and is wounding his wife's heart, Brad is currently trying to confront his frame of reference as hardly normal and challenge his expectations as unrealistic. Brad's wife doesn't need to kill herself trying to look like a supermodel. Instead, Brad needs to kill his idol.

I was recently challenged by a CD set I picked up from my local library entitled, *A Complaint Free World*. While I wasn't inclined to purchase and wear a purple reminder bracelet, I did find myself more cognizant of my conversation and the statements I uttered. I had to agree with the author that most people overestimate how positive they are and underestimate the frequency of their negative comments and complaints. Think about it. How many people do you think are going to say, "Yeah, on any given day, I'm a fairly negative person." Folks who think of themselves as pretty upbeat people are often embarrassed when I ask them, "When you are chatting with your coworkers about your company are the comments largely positive or critical?" One person remarked, "If you're asking if we get together and talk about how wonderful our idiotic boss is, the answer is no."

As I'm having a quiet lunch alone or writing in a coffee shop, I often cannot help but overhear the conversations next to me. Jesus said, "For where two or three come together in my name, there am I with them" (Matthew 18:20). He could have said, "Where two or more are gathered there is much complaining and griping." To the left of me two ladies are ripping on the doctor they work for about his "ridiculous policies" before moving on to education and bashing the school where their children are enrolled. Across from me are three guys who apparently work together in the same technology department. They are bonding via their vocal agreement about how lazy one of their colleagues is and how they repeatedly have to "cover his butt." Then one of the guys says, "I think he's milking this whole cancer thing for all it's worth." (I was wishing I had a Tazer.)

> The problem with complaining, however, is that it never changes anything.

If you don't want to listen to yourself just yet, listen to the conversations that people strike up with you and others. See if you notice the complaints about the gas prices, the traffic, their commute, the office, the company, upper management, their coworkers, the customers, the weather, the elections, the government, the Republicans, the Democrats, the economy, their aging parents, their unresponsive spouse, and their ungrateful-children-who-don't-know-how-good-they-got-it and are slobs-who-won't-lift-a-finger-to-help-around-the-house-cause-they'd-just-play-Xbox-all-day-if-I-let-them. Note the comments about other ethnic groups. Then there are the rude neighbors, the neighbor's dog, the Middle East, the housing market, the insurance and the health care system, the medication's side effects, the daughter's soccer coach, the messy house, the church's music, the senior pastor, the youth ministry, the lack of an emphasis on prayer, and another building program. Don't overlook the complaints about busyness, fatigue, and not enough sleep. Don't miss out on hearing what's wrong with America, the homeowner's association, today's teenagers, contemporary praise music, the recreation league director, the lawn, immigration laws, and the layout of the new grocery store.

But don't think that griping is a complete waste of time. Complaining actually serves many purposes:

1. *It enlists agreement.* It is not difficult to find someone who will tag team with you in a complaint match. Therefore common ground can be established quickly.
2. *It avoids taking action.* Talking negatively substitutes for taking positive action.
3. *It invites sympathy.* Yes, you poor dear, you are indeed over-worked, underpaid, unappreciated, misunderstood, mistreated, always sick, and never catch a break.
4. *It reduces expectations and accountability.* We demand less from people who are miserable. Complaining is an excellent method of keeping people's expectations of you to a minimum.

> Many people don't realize there is a limit to the helpfulness that talking about their problems can have if corresponding action isn't taken.

The problem with complaining, however, is that it never changes anything. Then again, maybe that's part of the attraction. I'm often asked as a counselor how I handle listening to people's problems all day. My response has always been that being fully present with troubled people who want to heal and to grow is not taxing. What does yank my drain plug and frustrate me are those who only desire agreement about how bad their life or marriage is. I'm able to identify them quickly because they keep showing me their "Yeah, but…" After a session or two of really seeking to hear someone's heart and their story, I'm ready to move on to the stage of helping the client respond in active and healthy ways to the problem.

I originally named my practice LifeChange Counseling Services because I make a basic assumption when an individual or couple comes to me for counseling—that there's something they want to change. They want to heal from a loss, break free from a stronghold, restore a relationship, cease a self-defeating behavior, or grow in their relationship with

God. They want to experience positive change. But the ones who moon me with their "Yeah, but…" resist interpreting their situation differently or taking any action.

Many people don't realize there is a limit to the helpfulness that talking about their problems can have if corresponding action isn't taken. The familiar bell-shaped curve applies here. As the line slopes upward along with the frequency/amount of disclosure, so increases the personal benefit of disclosure. Talking about it may bring relief, insight, clarity, and resolution. It may invite encouragement and support and spark brainstorming for solutions. Talking it out is highly recommended and is certainly therapeutic, much better than repression and stuffing it. But sometimes less is more. It is possible to take too many laxatives, if you know what I mean. At some point the slope of the bell-shaped relationship between the frequency of disclosure and helpfulness of disclosure peaks and then starts downward. How could that be? How could talking something out be counterproductive? It is because after the peak of helpful disclosure, continued talk (without positive action) becomes primarily a rehearsal and a repeat of previous statements. Often you'll notice that you're not saying anything new. You're repeating the same complaint to the same person and telling your same old story continually to new listeners. I'm not encouraging you to lie about how you're feeling or what's happening, but you don't need to repeatedly give the complete unabridged version of the story. And if you leave anything out regarding the current conditions, it's okay because you aren't under oath on a witness stand.

Language is fascinating in that it cannot be separated from thought. Try thinking without your silent language. Try saying anything without the split second of thought beforehand. But language and thought also work in another sequence as well. Not only does thought shape our speech, but speech (what we say or write) is found to shape our thoughts as well. Do you remember this trick when you were a kid?

"Hey, Tommy; say 'stop' seven times."
"Stop, stop, stop, stop, stop, stop, stop."

"What do you do you when you come to a green light?"

"Stop."

"Ha, ha, ha. No, bonehead. Green means go. Ha, ha, ha."

It's a dumb trick, but it actually illustrates the influence of repetitive speech on our brain.

Our ears aren't the only thing hearing what we say. Our minds are registering it too. And if speech shapes and reinforces our thoughts, do you see the implication of constant complaining and negative story-telling? Our spoken words, positive or negative, influence and instruct our minds.

Paul understood the power of what we dwell on. Perhaps that's why he wrote this exhortation to the Philippians:

> Summing it all up, friends, I'd say you'll do best by filling your minds and meditating on things true, noble, reputable, authentic, compelling, gracious—the best, not the worst; the beautiful, not the ugly; things to praise, not things to curse. (Philippians 4:8, MSG)

A profound truth I readily admit is elusive to me is the idea that I have considerable control over my thoughts. I often act like my brain is a hotel where any thought with a credit card can get a room. While my mind will resist blatant statements or opinions I clearly disagree with, the subtle ones are sneaky, dressing up like reasonable thoughts and blending right in. The guards at the gate rarely recognize them as impostors and enemies of peace, joy, and contentment.

In Paul's letter to the Colossians he uses the phrase "set your minds" (Colossians 3:2). You have likely worked in an office where your computer is part of a network. There may be several printers in your department that you can print to, but when you command your computer to print it will automatically send the document to the default printer. Let's say your default printer is a black ink only printer right outside your office, but you want to print out a document in color. The color printer is downstairs but is still connected in the network to your computer. To print your project on that color printer you just have to click on your printer settings and select the desired printer from the options. You're now ready to print in color. It's not hard, but you do have to consciously and intentionally reset your desired printer for the color project. Likewise, there are places our mind instinctively goes. As if to a default printer, there are thoughts and words that are almost automatically produced. But too often we act like the default printer, the one most familiar, is the only printer available to us. There is another option, but we will have to choose it...over and over again.

Paul proposes that truly spiritual people are positive people. But wait a minute. Being spiritually alert and sensitive often means that you're also more aware of what's wrong with the world. With a heightened commitment to justice and compassion, your antennae are up for signs of injustice and oppression. When you are true to a moral code, it's hard not to notice the rampant displays of immorality and depravity. Part of what it means to adhere to Jesus' command to be salt and light in the culture is to be different and to make a difference. Often that means speaking up when something isn't right.

But that is no invitation to be mean-spirited. Paul reminds us, "In your anger do not sin" (Ephesians 4:26). It is possible to disagree, protest, and stand firm (in a relationship or in an opposing culture) while still being respectful. While we are not to be empty plates for whatever ideology or immorality the world dishes out, we are not excused to spew verbal venom at those who oppose us.

Paul uses the metaphor "shine like stars in the universe" (Philippians 2:15) in the context of warning against complaining and arguing. Paul suggests that when we refrain from chronic complaining and arguing (which is the cultural norm and a tendency of human nature), then we will stand out like bright stars against a backdrop of darkness. It is a paradox that Christians are called to feel the least at home here on this earth and in this life, and yet we are to be the most joyful while we are here.

12

There's Rat Poop in My Corn Dog!

I have these two plastic sticks that serve as fences in the grocery line. They clearly define what I've chosen and what I will pay for. I did not choose canned artichoke hearts—that's yours. For the person in front of me, my fence is a boundary of ownership and choice and a way of saying, "Relax, lady, I know that's your Haagen Dazs."

For the guy behind me, I put my fence down as a way of saying, "Don't crowd my stuff," and in case anyone is looking, the case of Coors Light is not mine. (I have corralled my choices.)

But when I get to the cashier I find there are items in my collection I did not choose.

Difficult and painful things I did not select. Stressors I do not want.

I had no buy-one-get-one-free coupon for some of this mess. I don't want it. I did not pluck it from the shelf and put it in my cart. However, it is mine now. It is not the life of the lady in front of me; it is not the life of the guy behind me. It's mine.

God, help me with the cost of these things I did not choose. Help me carry these plastic bags of stuff I did not want.

(August 23, journal entry)

D ad, what's this in my corn dog?" It was the corn dog that I pulled from the package in the freezer and baked at 350 degrees for the prescribed length of time. Not a nutritious lunch, but my eight-year-old son Trevor liked them. Trevor walked toward me with that expression on his face like crinkled up paper, holding out the half-eaten dog.

It didn't take a magnifying glass to see something black, about the size of a jelly bean, with disconcerting texture, lodged between the pink meat and the pale yellow cornmeal. Actually, the offensive look-ing material was not completely intact; in his chomp Trevor had sliced off and eaten some of the mystery thing. But there was plenty left and the sight of the remainder along with the thought of Trevor having ingested a portion of that thing made me a bit queasy. Not wanting to cause an immediate gag reflex in Trevor, I just said, "I'm not sure what that is, Son; let me fix you something else for lunch." I chose not to tell him that I thought he had possibly bitten off and swallowed a piece of rat poop.

"Tell you what, I'll slip out and get you a Happy Meal." I start gathering things up to go out. Stay calm. No sudden moves. I watched Trevor closely for any signs of rodent poop-related illness. When Dorrie got home I took her aside and proceeded with show-and-tell. Eeeeeww-wwww," she said. "My thoughts exactly," I replied. "And Trevor swal-lowed the other half of *that*, whatever *that* is." Even though neither one of us had much experience with mice droppings, we thought it probably looked something like *that*.

How did this gastro drama turn out? Well, Trevor is still alive, and at age sixteen shows no ill effects from having swallowed a piece of...cara-melized and charred cornmeal. I'm fully aware that I often respond to problems as if they were some disturbing foreign substance that should not be in my life in the first place. And I don't want God to just remove the problem. In my less healthy moments I think I expect some kind of apology for its being there in the first place. "I'm so sorry, Ramon. I don't know how this eluded the inspectors. We'll take care of it. How can we make it up to you?" I don't suffer well.

Why do we, Americans especially, suffer so poorly? I think it's because we expect life to be quite manageable. We expect to get what we want, when we want it. Any pain is to be prevented, relieved, or eliminated. No wonder we treat hardship like a foreign substance. Peter took a very different approach to suffering. When he wrote 1 Peter, his audience was suffering some of the worse persecution in the history of the faith. These Christians were being persecuted by none other than the monstrous Nero. He threw Christians to the lions for the entertainment of the masses. He lit one of his gardens with Christians burning at the stake. It was to those Christians and their families that Peter wrote, "Dear friends, do not be surprised at the painful trial you are suffering, as though something strange were happening to you" (1 Peter 4:12).

> We set ourselves up for much disappointment and frustration by expecting life, God, and others to cooperate with our feel-good plan.

Peter exhorts his readership to put their suffering in perspective. Your afflictions are not unique, and you have not been singled out for unusual and exceptional pain. Don't be surprised by suffering, Peter says. Expect such things. The refusal to accept the validity of pain certainly does not dull it, but rather sharpens its edge. We set ourselves up for much disappointment and frustration by expecting life, God, and others to cooperate with our feel-good plan.

WHAT DID YOU EXPECT?

As a marriage therapist I repeatedly witness the power of expectations, including unspoken ones, unfulfilled ones, and unrealistic ones. As an exercise in premarital counseling I often have a couple take a sheet a paper and write "My Expectations" at the top. Then I instruct them to write out all their expectations of their partner and of marriage. Most will pause and then write something about expecting faithfulness and fidelity. Then writer's block immediately sets in and they do that dart-

> We walk in our relationship with God carrying a backpack full of our expectations, not fully conscious of most of them.

ing of the eyes around the ceiling thing, as if hints from prior couples were scribbled up there. Then I seize the opportunity to tell them their response is typical and that in fact we most often discover what our expectations are when they are not met. Our reactions (disappointment, irritation, hurt, anger) let us know that we've just unearthed another subtle expectation. The expectations have been there for a long time, but most landmines are not discovered by metal detectors but by unfortunate stepping.

We not only bring our subtle expectations to the table of marriage, but to all relationships—those with our parents, our children, our extended family, friends, neighbors, employers, employees, coworkers, etc. In fact, you name any relationship and there are subtle expectations attached to it. It's not any different in our relationship with God. We walk in our relationship with God carrying a backpack full of our expectations, not fully conscious of most of them, almost as though someone else packed it for us. We certainly don't recall selecting our expectations from a myriad of shelved options and bagging them for the journey. Not to stretch the metaphor too far, but I think it's safe to say that we've been carrying these expectations for so long that the weight is familiar and we've grown accustomed to the slower pace—and the duller spirit—that the weight requires. Unrealistic expectations prolong suffering and cause joy to be very elusive. Let's explore a few of the most prevalent—and most dangerous—unrealistic expectations.

We Expect Immunity from Suffering

My friend, who holds a black belt in karate, describes the day he learned how to defend against someone attacking with a knife. The instructor demonstrated how to use their legs and forearms to take the nonlethal cuts before either escaping or defeating the attacker. Tom interrupted the instructor, "Excuse me, but I'd like to know how to avoid being cut at all!" The instructor replied, "Tommy, this isn't Hollywood. When you are being attacked by someone with a knife you *will* be cut. Once you accept being cut, you can then concentrate on not being killed." But don't we all silently expect a privileged immunity from crisis and suffering as one of the perks of being a faithful devotee to God and a really good person? We expect to avoid being cut. Note the sufferings of Paul recorded in 2 Corinthians 11:23–28:

- Five times he endured the "forty lashes minus one."
- Three times he was beaten with rods.
- He was tortured by stoning.
- Three times he was shipwrecked.
- He spent twenty-four hours treading water in the ocean.
- He faced danger in rivers, in the sea, in the country, and in the city.
- He faced danger from bandits, Jews, Gentiles, and from false brothers.
- He was deprived of food, water, shelter, clothing, and sleep.

That's not the kind of experience that makes the recruiting poster. Furthermore, if anyone in Paul's day had reason to expect that faithfulness and obedience might exempt him from suffering, it was Paul. But that was one expectation that didn't bulk his baggage. Paul trusted Christ when he said, "Here on earth you will have many trials and sorrows. But take heart, because I have overcome the world" (John 16:33 NLT). A joyful life is not one void of pain and suffering. Author and theologian Dr. Lewis Smedes explains that "if our joy is honest joy, it must be somehow congruous with human tragedy. This is the test of joy's integrity; is it compatible with pain? Only the heart that hurts has a right to joy."[23]

Popular Carnegie Mellon professor, Randy Pausch, became known to the world with the presentation and publication of *The Last Lecture*. Dying with pancreatic cancer Pausch delivered not a final lecture morbidly focused on his pending death but one celebrating the life lessons learned in the journey. While watching a television special about Pausch and his family, I could not help but observe that his lovely wife, Jai, was quite remarkable herself, striving for peace and even joy despite her hurting heart. In the crucible of cancer's death sentence on her husband, she juggled love, grief, acceptance, anger, and savoring. She reported that one of the mantras that she frequently repeats to herself is "I have everything I need." It reminded me of David writing in the Psalms, "The LORD is my shepherd; I have all that I need" (Psalm 23:1 NLT). The "everything" is much more than an assurance of material provision. It is the confidence that God will supply my emotional and spiritual needs when I need them.

> For Paul it made all the difference, knowing that God was in him, with him, and for him. He trusted that anything God allowed past the gatekeepers and into his life was an event or a condition that he would be given the grace to handle.

With a clearer spiritual context, the apostle Paul declares, "I can do all things through Christ who strengthens me." Paul is saying, "I can handle everything that comes my way because I know that I'm not alone." For Paul it made all the difference, knowing that God was in him, with him, and for him. He trusted that anything God allowed past the gatekeepers and into his life was an event or a condition that he would be given the grace to handle. As someone who will get a sinus infection before a major speaking gig and act as though God fell asleep on the job, I'm simultaneously inspired and challenged by Paul's conviction.

We Expect to Know Why Our Suffering Occurs

If God does allow my suffering, then I want an explanation! Sometimes we think that eventually we'll understand why, when in fact, the *why* question is seldom answered. Others will speculate upon our case, and we ourselves will hypothesize, but ultimately we have no confirmation of our theories. As Scripture says, "Now we see through a glass, darkly" (1 Corinthians 13:12 KJV) or as it is paraphrased in *The Message*: "We don't yet see things clearly. We're squinting in a fog, peering through a mist." Besides, the *why* question is not really an intellectual inquiry that would be satisfied with facts. Rather, it is an emotional question that seeks reassurance and comfort. Answers seldom bring healing. To review *why* questions, re-read chapter 6.

> At times we want to say to God, "You shouldn't have made this mess, but since you did, you better clean it up quickly."

We Expect and Require that Suffering Be Alleviated

A lot of once-religious people have put God on probation because he's not doing his job to prevent suffering, or at least bring quick relief. When the Exxon tanker *Valdez* spilled its oil off the coast of Alaska in 1989, the U.S. government penalized the company for making the mess in the first place, and then punished them again for not cleaning it up fast enough. At times we want to say to God, "You shouldn't have made this mess, but since you did, you better clean it up quickly." Discovering you have a deadly disease like cancer can make you wonder why God did not prevent it, and enduring the treatments only to have the cancer return often provokes us to ask God why he did not bring healing. Christian psychologist Larry Crabb makes the following challenging assessment:

> We treat personal discomfort as the central evil from which we need to be saved. When we blend the pursuit of comfort with Christianity, Jesus becomes a divine masseur whose demands we heed only after we are properly relaxed. But that is not the Christianity of the Bible. Christ offers hope, not relief, in the middle of

suffering, and he commands us to pursue him hotly even when we'd rather stop and look after our own well-being.[24]

When faced with execution in a blazing furnace, Shadrach, Meshach, and Abednego declared to King Nebuchadnezzar that God was able to save them from the flames, but even if God chose not to rescue them, they would still worship him and would accept death rather than bow to the king's idols (Daniel 3:17–18). What an incredible statement of trust—circumstances and outcomes did not determine their allegiance and worship. I yearn to get to that solid place where I choose God regardless of the circumstances God allows. I'm not there yet.

*   *   *

I once counseled a father who refused to accept his daughter's interracial engagement and approaching wedding. The young man's outstanding qualities were irrelevant to him. So blinded by his racism, so offended by his grown daughter's choice of a life mate, the father rejected his daughter entirely and resented his wife for not taking his side The young couple was not welcome in his home, and he boycotted the wedding. His blindness to his sin hurt his daughter tremendously and wedged a divide between him and his wife that eventually widened to a chasm of divorce.

At one point prior to the wedding I said to this man, "So, let me get this straight, you're going to allow something or someone your daughter chooses to determine whether or not you choose her. You're going to reject her as your daughter because of whom she loves and wants to marry. Is that right?" "Well, she rejected me first! She knew before she ever went out with this guy how I feel about white girls hooking up with blacks. It's almost like she did this to spite me!" His statements and his anger reflected his obvious racist core attitude about black people in general, not just interracial relationships. However, I knew it would be useless in this conversation to confront that. "So, your daughter is going to marry a black man just so she can tick you off, huh? Is that what you think?"

"She knows it makes me mad," he argued. "Yeah, but she would have to really despise you, really hate you, in order to be willing to sacrifice her life and future by marrying someone she doesn't love just to punish you. Do you really think your daughter dislikes you that much? She doesn't. In fact, she loves you in spite of how you're treating her. She's not trying to defy you by marrying this guy. She wishes you would walk her down the aisle and give her away. She craves your blessing, but she won't be manipulated by your choice to withhold it."

The father never seemed to grasp that his love for his daughter was utterly conditional. It seemed so obvious and absurd in its human form. Yet, I see people do that with God all the time. God's approval ratings rise and fall with favorable or unfavorable circumstances. The choices of whether to actively engage God, talk to God, believe God, trust God, and worship God, are all tethered to what life events God has permitted or ordained in the realm of personal experience. *What God does or does not permit for me will determine whether I choose him or not.* We would never proclaim that on a bumper sticker or have it cross-stitched on a pillow, but that is how most of us operate.

I just need to ask: Who keeps coming up with these corny, trite sayings for display on church signs? Are these in a book somewhere? I know we live in a world of sound bites, but does the church in America really believe that the way to reach their community is with pithy quotes like "God answers knee-mail"? Recently I came across the roadside sign of a nearby church which read: "Try Jesus. Results Guaranteed." I'm confident that Jesus is delighted to know that he is being touted like an effective underarm deodorant or lawn fertilizer. But what happens if I try Jesus and don't get the results I am looking for? I'm sure as heck not walking willingly into the furnace fires of martyrdom to stick up for a God who won't even heal my acid reflux. In church, instead of singing (without really believing) the words of the hymn "Trust and Obey," perhaps we should collectively sing to God the Janet Jackson hit, "What Have You Done for Me Lately?"

13

God Still Invites You to Dream Big

W hen will my life not suck?" It's a question we ask when we feel the world closing in, when our efforts seem vain, and when our circle of influence seems to be shrinking rather than expanding. Christ came so that you might have abundance, not scarcity. He came so that your world might grow and stretch and so that you might grow and stretch with it.

JOSHUA 17:14-18

It was one of the biggest grand-opening celebrations ever. Forty years after the exodus from Egypt, the Israelites completed history's longest walkathon through the desert where they experienced every trial and affliction imaginable. Now they are at the ribbon cutting—the door of the Promised Land. Following the conquests and the beginning of settlement in Canaan, one of the twelve tribes came to Joshua and said, "Why did you give us only one allotment of land? We have many people because the Lord has greatly blessed us" (v. 14). Joshua replied, "You do have a lot of people. Go out to the forested region and clear it if the hill country of Ephraim is too small for you" (v. 15, author's paraphrase).

One of the fascinating things about this exchange is what Joshua does not say. Joshua leads the people into the Promised Land, and like a real estate developer, he distributes new subdivisions among the inhabitants. This is a sweet real estate deal—no loan applications, no thirty-year mortgage payments, and no closing costs. Of course, you'll have to build your own house, but there will be no property taxes based on location and square footage. What more could you ask for? Well, Joseph's people ask for more land. You halfway expect Joshua to say, "You ungrateful, greedy people! Bunch of whiners—'we need more land, we need more land.' You should be thankful for what I gave you. Get out of here before I change my mind and give you a trailer park next to the airport!" But Joshua doesn't say that. He doesn't rebuke them for being greedy or lecture them about contentment. Instead he says, "If you want more land you can have it. Take your axes and chainsaws and clear the trees in the forested region over there."

> Christ came so that you might have abundance, not scarcity. He came so that your world might grow and stretch and so that you might grow and stretch with it.

To the descendants of Joseph this is good news and bad news. The good news is that they can have a big plot of land. Then they bring up what they don't like about the plan. "Umm, the place you're talking about with all the trees…it's a real nice spot, but there's a bunch of people living there already and they're mean and very strong. We don't think they're real open to relocating." Joshua responds to this new complaint with calm encouragement. "You have many people and great strength.

You will not have just one lot in the hill country, but the forested region as well. Clear it and its farthest regions will be yours. You can drive out the Canaanites, even though they are strong and have weapons."

Your life doesn't have to suck. You don't have to settle for a small portion—a cramped little piece of real estate where you don't have room to stretch your legs. If you want more land, it's quite possible that you can have it. I'm not preaching the prosperity gospel here. I'm not equating more land with wealth. I am equating land with an expansion of opportunity and influence for something much more profound than selfish gain. I'm talking about more territory to fulfill your calling! More elbow room to do good, make a difference, and help others. God may choose to bless your business and thus allow you to channel more resources to places of need. Nevertheless, never be misguided into thinking that one of the main reasons that God may choose to bless you is so you can hear the cash register sing. I have unapologetically asked God to bless my efforts as an author, but not for the sake of sales and royalties. I write because I'm passionate about a message that I feel must be told. I'm a writer and a counselor for much the same reason—I get a buzz from helping people. It is a great privilege to connect through writing with people I'll never meet. Getting paid for it is a bonus.

The apostle Paul said, "I am compelled to preach" (1 Corinthians 9:16). Well, I am compelled to write—to encourage, comfort, strengthen, inspire, and challenge. So why shouldn't I ask God for an ever-increasing platform for my writing and speaking? Assuming that I don't become prideful and get too big for my britches, what is the problem with God granting me a larger audience for truth telling and encouragement? Joseph's descendants' petition for more territory was not presumptuous. Don't think for a moment that God owes you something. This request was not expressed with a spirit of entitlement. The spokesman acknowledged that their high census numbers for the group were because the Lord has blessed them. This was not a people who had forgotten the source of their blessing. Nor had they become greedy and unappreciative. Theirs was a declaration of fact (we're going to be extremely crowded) and a plea for consideration (we need more land).

If You Want the Land, You've Got to Clear Some Trees

While Joseph's initial property allotment in the hill country didn't sound too difficult to settle and develop, making a subdivision out of the forested region would be no easy task unless they wanted to live in tree houses. To live in the bonus region would require time, muscle, and sweat. There's nothing all that spiritual about logging. There are no deep hidden secrets to success here. You want to live here in the forested region? Swing an ax!

Clearing the trees is simply consistent effort and hard work, especially if it is largely a solo project. I'll use again the example of writing. Forgive me for stating the obvious, but writers write. For an aspiring author clearing the trees means B.I.C.H.O.K.—butt in chair, hands on keyboard. Real writers write while wannabe writers fantasize about being an author. Wannabe writers think about writing, read about writing, talk about writing, go to conferences about writing—almost everything except actually writing. Real writers get ink on the page, lots of ink on reams of paper. There is no substitute for putting in the extended time and prolonged effort that is required to advance your cause.

If You Really Want the Land, You Must Drive out the Canaanites

Okay, let's be clear that this has nothing to do with stepping on people who get in your way or even beating the competition. Driving out the Canaanites is a spiritual battle. In the Old Testament the actual battles with the barbaric inhabitants of the land had a double meaning, similar to the double meaning of the Narnia Chronicles, especially *The Lion, the Witch, and the Wardrobe.* These historical Old Testament battles also symbolize our ongoing struggles with an Adversary that opposes us at every turn. Dedicated to the erosion of our morals and the implosion of our morale, this enemy is referred to by Jesus as a thief who comes to steal and kill and destroy (John 10:10) and by the apostle Peter as a roaring lion on the prowl, looking for someone to devour (1 Peter 5:8). It is this spiritual reality that prompted Paul to remind the Ephesians that "we are not fighting against flesh-and-blood enemies, but against evil rulers and authorities of the unseen world, against mighty powers in this dark world, and against evil spirits in the heavenly places" (Ephesians 6:12 NLT). It is a battle for our souls, our hearts, our dreams, our relationships, our peace and joy, our life mission, and even our legacy. Much is at stake; do not be naïve about the opposition.

> What if being a special instrument means actually becoming a less visible instrument?

Paul's letter to Timothy makes an astute observation about our potential in light of our battle: "In a wealthy home some utensils are made of gold and silver, and some are made of wood and clay. The expensive utensils are used for special occasions, and the cheap ones are for everyday use. If you keep yourself pure, you will be a special utensil for honorable use. Your life will be clean, and you will be ready for the Master to use you for every good work" (2 Timothy 2:20–21 NLT).

Paul reminds us that we have considerable influence in the scope and reach of our mission. This is not so much God rewarding good behavior like a parent taking a child to the ice cream parlor for a good report card, but rather it's a releasing of significant assignments to those he considers trustworthy. Note that upgraded assignments do not necessarily mean flashier assignments with more staff, a newer building, or a bigger budget. What if being a special instrument means actually becoming a less visible instrument? Significant work is often unrecognized and unrewarded. Mother Teresa did not go to Calcutta because God hinted that her behind-the-scenes work with the poor would one day net her a Noble Peace Prize and worldwide notoriety. She remained true to her calling because she felt that the mission of mercy among the poor, the sick, the dying, the alienated, and the condemned was her special appointment.

It was God who made her a special instrument decades before international media tried to anoint her.

That we are even candidates for special designation is the work of grace, and yet there is a responsibility on our part to be qualified for the honor. And there is no competing against others for a few choice spots on the all-star team. The appointments are not made based on comparisons, but are based on the Lord's gracious choice. Paul, who was more blown away by being a recipient of grace than anyone, nevertheless was alert to the sneaky traps of disqualification. He was vigilant in discipline and self-control, declaring that "after I have preached to others, I myself will not be disqualified for the prize" (1 Corinthians 9:27). In blunt terms, Paul did not want to work so hard for so long and then blow it by doing something stupid. Pastors, politicians, and athletes alike have had hidden sins publicly exposed, ruining their careers and credibility, overshadowing their good deeds and accomplishments, and in many cases destroying their families.

It may seem that many people are quite content with their little half-acre plot in Canaan. But then I think about their wishes and complaints, how they think their life would be better or complete if they only had _____. This is not true contentment but a counterfeit contentment laced with complacency and fatalism. It is a resolved discontent. Life sucks but, hey, what can I do about it?

VISION SABOTEURS

It's disappointing to see people of faith act like the most complacent and fatalistic humans on the planet. I see them using one or both of two spiritual-sounding rationales for their lethargy: "This is just my cross to bear" and "This world is not my home." Most of the time when I hear these pious sounding sentiments the speaker has a faulty perspective, which leads to wrong actions (or no actions). That person is growing into a tree that sports plenty of foliage but little, if any, fruit that feeds others.

"Spiritual" Rationale 1: This Is Just My Cross to Bear

When Jesus said to his followers "take up your cross daily and follow me" (Luke 9:23) he didn't say "carry the cross life hands to you." Your financial crisis is not your cross to bear. Neither is a physical condition, a family problem, or a lousy job. Difficult life circumstances are not crosses to bear. Volitionally taking up the cross (an emblem of death) is a declaration that I'm crucifying my demand, my requirement to have my own way. It is a decision of self-sacrifice, a daily battle against the demon of selfishness. Don't confuse this with a self-loathing statement such as, "I'm not important. It doesn't matter what I want."

> Taking up the cross is a voluntary identification with Christ that may not make you very popular.

Taking up the cross is a voluntary identification with Christ that may not make you very popular. In the West that affiliation probably won't get you tortured or killed; it is more likely to cause you to be regarded with amusement or disrespect for your quaint beliefs and outdated worldviews. In many countries, however, the bravely chosen affinity with Christ can carry a death sentence. What we call religious persecution in America is laughable and would be insulting to the world's true martyrs, except they are too humble and too preoccupied to concern themselves with petty insults.

Correctly defining "cross to bear" is not just a matter of semantics, given the fact that bad theology usually becomes bad biography. In other words, what we believe (whether it is true or false) influences our decisions and actions. One of the problems with claiming a life struggle as our cross is that we are then prone to insist that carrying it is all that can or should be expected of us. Consequently, we don't really have anything to offer anyone, because our energy is used up just holding up our burdensome wooden life. We can't really experience any joy in life, not with this heavy beam practically digging a hole in our shoulder.

And you'll notice that people who carry life crosses don't do it very quietly. They often like to remind us of the weight they are transporting daily, a report that is designed to elicit admiration, sympathy, or both. It also wards off expectations. If I've already got a bad back from carrying this cross, surely you wouldn't expect me to help you move furniture.

Not only do I fortress myself from the expectations of others, but I also shrink or cast aside any lofty expectations I have or once had for myself. Not only do my expectations go out the window, so do my hopes and aspirations. But as much as we are prone to that complacency and fatalism, we are usually inspired by true stories of common people who have overcome seemingly insurmountable odds to not just survive but thrive. Those stories become best sellers because we desperately want to believe that we too can overcome obstacles. The reason that a survivor story does more than just entertain us is that it inspires the possibility of the survivor's story somehow being our own. As if the indefatigable human spirit were something brokered, we wonder if we might qualify for the loan.

Do we imagine that God wants to keep us beaten down so that we'll stay humble and dependent? Humility and dependence on God are outstanding qualities to be sure, but God does not desire for us to wallow hopelessly in our misery to squeeze out those qualities. How does it glorify God that his followers are miserable and despairing, shipwrecked glooms who are just treading water until they are rescued by death and uploaded to heaven? Remember what Paul says: "We now have this light shining in our hearts, but we ourselves are like fragile clay jars containing this great treasure. This makes it clear that our great power is from God, not from ourselves" (2 Corinthians 4:7 NLT). Paul is declaring that God has poured extraordinary potential and promise into very ordinary containers. Jesus said we are to be light in a dark world. I think that means being candles, flashlights, searchlights, spotlights, lighthouses, and front porch lights—every kind of positive light needed by a dimly lit culture of people with major hurts and miniscule hope. If we are so preoccupied with the splinters from our supposed cross bearing, we'll ignore the deeper emotional, spiritual, and relational wounds carved into the souls of those around us. Jesus will have taught us the parable of the good Samaritan with no effect.

"Spiritual" Rationale 2: This Earth Is Not My Home

Our human life in these earth suits is incredibly brief in light of eternity. The Scriptures remind us of the transient nature of life and the hope of heaven. Ultimately human suffering must take into account the edict that this life is not all there is. Sometimes it is the only thing that makes a season of great suffering bearable or makes our existence something not merely cruel or unfortunate. Have you ever felt such despair that you wished that you could die? Even though you would not manipulate your own death, you put out a welcome mat for it. Often the greater courage is seen not in those who will resist death but in those who will not invite it.

> If we are so preoccupied with the splinters from our supposed cross bearing, we'll ignore the deeper emotional, spiritual, and relational wounds carved into the souls of those around us.

The overdone earth-is-not-my-home mentality not only leads to poor stewardship and irresponsible management of a planet with limited resources, it can also produce the complacency of tourists who feels no sense of responsibility for contributing anything of value to their surroundings. After all, they're just passing through. This mentality is like viewing life as a rental car. No one washes and waxes a rental car—a customer is just borrowing the car, therefore maintenance is not their concern or responsibility. But neither the planet, nor your community, or your life is a rented vehicle. While you're here you have responsibility for what's entrusted to you. The parable of the talents (Matthew 25:14–30) reminds us that we are all stewards and not renters. God's message through the parable is that there is great responsibility, as well as great opportunity. Why decline the invitation to make your life extraordinary? Again, that has nothing to do with becoming wealthy, famous, or powerful, but it has everything to do with reducing the weight of your unsightly complaints and excuses and making your days here count. Furthermore, life can be enjoyable. The earth-is-not-my-home mantra can also foster a false belief that God doesn't want me to enjoy my life here. Since God doesn't want me to get attached to this

> Often the greater courage is seen not in those who will resist death but in those who will not invite it.

world, doesn't want me to lose focus on the eternal, then while he's likely to meet my most basic needs, he's not going to endorse unnecessary luxuries and unproductive frivolity.

America has benefited greatly from its Puritan work ethic that was laid as a foundation in the nation's infancy. If there's a spiritual weak spot in that ethic, it's that the spiritual life is all about discipline and productivity and not intimacy, enjoyment, passion, creativity, humor, or entertainment. In its flight from worldly hedonism the church can run right off the opposite cliff of asceticism. It is a drab and scratchy wardrobe of Christianity that denies the legitimate enjoyment of what God has created. I mean, come on! Would God really want you to take a drawing class at the arts center just because you wanted to? Don't you need a better reason than that? Could God possibly endorse you visiting a region of the world you've always longed to see unless it was during a mission trip? Hmmmmm?

A VISION FOR YOUR LIFE

I remember comedienne Lily Tomlin saying, "I always wanted to be somebody, but now I realize I should have been more specific." A friend of mine has inspired me to develop a fifty by fifty list—fifty things I want to accomplish or experience by age fifty. (I'm a few months from turning forty-nine so I'm thinking of making it a twenty-five by fifty list.) Because of the exercise I am asking what I want to be true about me and about my life, for which fifty is just a measuring stick. As Andy Stanley is fond of saying, "Everybody ends up somewhere in life. Don't you want to end up somewhere on purpose?"[25]

I've always liked the analogy that one of my seminary professors used to describe God's sovereignty. The passengers on a cruise ship do not dictate its course, ports, or ultimate destination. The captain does. But the passengers have quite a bit of freedom on the ship to move about, make choices, and enjoy the experience. They can maximize their on-board experiences and ports-of-call visits, mismanage them, or totally waste them. With their ticket they purchased the right to choose and the responsibility to choose well. I am choosing to adjust my thinking and live my life in such a way that when I get ready to disembark at the end of the journey I won't be saying, "Well, that really sucked!" I intend to go down the stairs to the dock saying what I did when I got out of the passenger's seat of a race car that had just topped 160 mph around the Charlotte Motor Speedway: "Now that was an awesome ride!"

Notes

1. Larry Crabb, *Inside Out* (Colorado Springs: NavPress, 1988), 17.

2. John Piper is an extraordinary thinker and writer in his thorough treatment of finding our delight in the glories and mysteries of God. I commend to you Piper's *Desiring God* (Multnomah Books, 2003) and *When I Don't Desire God: How to Fight for Joy* (Crossway Books, 2004).

3. Frederick Buechner, *The Sacred Journey: A Memoir of Early Days* (San Francisco: Harper & Row, 1982), 6.

4. Tim Hansel, *You Gotta Keep Dancin'* (Elgin, IL: David C. Cook, 1985), 26.

5. In addition to hearing Dave Busby speak on several occasions, I once hosted him for an event at my church, which gave me the privilege to spend some quality time alone with him and become well-acquainted with this amazing man. Dave passed away in 1997 at the age of 46 from medical complications. I'm hard pressed to improve upon the description of him from his posthumous website (www.davebusby.com): "Dave Busby was a mystery. He managed to live a life completely given to God, pumping with energy and passion for young people. In the midst of daily, mammoth struggles with cystic fibrosis, polio, liver disease, heart disease, and diabetes, Dave went down deep in his life with God and he came up strong in order to bring others into the same deep and intimate relationship he had with Jesus."

6. Larry Crabb, *Connecting* (Nashville: Word, Nashville, 1997), 43.

7. Tal Ben-Shahar, *Happier* (New York: McGraw Hill, New York, 2007), 120-121.

8. Kathrin Chavez, "May I Have the Envelope Please?" *The Tennessean*, October 8, 2004.

9. Mosaic, "About," http://mosaic.org/about/.

10. M. Scott Peck, *The Road Less Traveled* (New York: Simon & Schuster, 1978), 15.

11. Brennan Manning, *Ruthless Trust* (San Francisco: Harper Collins, 2000), 150.

12. Gerald Sittser, *A Grace Disguised: How the Soul Grows through Loss* (Grand Rapids: Zondervan, 2004), 45-46.

13. Calvin Miller, *Walking With Saints: Through the Best and Worst Times of Our Lives* (Nashville: Thomas Nelson, 1995), 173.

14. Calvin Miller, *Walking With Saints*, 199.

15. Emily Perl Kingsley, "Welcome to Holland," ©1987 by Emily Perl Kingsley. All rights reserved. Reprinted by permission of the author.

16. John Eldredge, *The Journey of Desire* (Nashville: Thomas Nelson, 2000), 182.

17. Robert McCammon, *Boy's Life* (New York: Pocket Books, 1991), 3.

18. Archibald Hart, *The Anxiety Cure* (Nashville: Word Publishing, 1999), 6.

19. William Backus & Marie Chapin, *Telling Yourself the Truth* (Minneapolis: Bethany House, 1980), 68.

20. *Merriam-Webster's Collegiate Dictionary*, 11th ed., s.v. "Worry."

21. Stanley Baldwin, *Bruised But Not Broken* (Portland: Multnomah, 1985), pp. 79-85.

22. Calvin Miller, *The Singer* (Chicago: Intervarsity Press, 1975), 142.

23. Lewis Smedes, *How Can It Be All Right When Everything is Wrong?* (New York: Harper & Row, 1982), 15.

24. Larry Crabb, *Finding God* (Grand Rapids: Zondervan, 1993), 36.

25. Andy Stanley, *Visioneering* (Portland: Multnomah, 1999), 9-12.

HELLSING ①